7611

CARS – DRIVEN BY DESIGN

Sports Cars from the 1950s to the 1970s

Edited by
Barbara Til and
Dieter Castenow

KUNST PALAST

HIRMER

CONTENTS

PREFACE

FELIX KRÄMER

Over the past one hundred and thirty years, the automobile has become a symbol of modern life. It both expresses and symbolises individuality and freedom and goes far beyond its practical utility: it combines technology and mobility as well as the art and cultural history of the twentieth century. The ecstatic proclamation by the artist André Derain – 'My Bugatti is more beautiful than any work of art' – at the end of the 1920s demonstrates the enthusiasm this technological achievement triggered, and quite a few people saw the emergence of art rooted in the aesthetic of industrial products. No design object shaped the twentieth century as significantly as the car.

It is therefore all the more surprising that the aesthetic dimension of the automobile is given hardly any attention in the presentations and collections held by art and design museums. The Museum of Modern Art in New York was one of the few institutions to initiate exhibitions of cars shortly after World War Two and to include select vehicles such as the Cisitalia 202 Coupé and the Jaguar E-type in its collections. The first automobile exhibition at MoMA opened in 1951 under the plain title *8 Automobiles*. Its programmatic goal was nothing less than to put the aesthetic, artistic design of cars at its centre: "automobiles are hollow, rolling sculptures" reads the first sentence of the catalogue. Eight vehicles – sports cars and limousines – were presented, individually, on low marble pedestals. We too have put the vehicles on pedestals, like statues, in order to sensitise the visitor to the aesthetic dimension of these objects, which are designed with such attention to detail. However, unlike our colleagues at MoMA, we are not exhibiting any cars from our own day. We are aware that such an exhibition would be a wholly different project today, since the conventional combustion engine is increasingly a thing of the past, but also because in times of self-driving cars and the complete gridlock in urban centres, there has been a fundamental change in our relationship to mobility.

CARS – Driven by Design will be the first exhibition of automobiles at the Kunstpalast. The focus is on sports cars from the 1950s to the 1970s that set the standards in automobile design. The canon of forms that was developed during this period still informs the appearance of our vehicles today. The desire for renewal was expressed particularly clearly in the exclusive sports-car segment of the market, since here designers were given a greater freedom for their creativity than in other areas, and the aesthetics of design became a central concern.

The decision to present such an automobile exhibition at the Kunstpalast deliberately directs visitors' attention to an important part of the museum's collection that has been given less attention in recent decades. In addition to painting, sculpture, prints and glass works, the

Kunstpalast is home to an outstanding design collection. This breadth must be highlighted more than it has been, and topics for special exhibitions will be developed with this in mind. Devoting an exhibition to the most successful design object of the twentieth century is part of this. In doing so, it is important for the Kunstpalast to contribute to a growing awareness of our surroundings – to open the public's eyes to the aesthetic power of art and design.

The fact that we have managed to represent this theme with outstanding sports cars from automobile history is primarily down to the generosity of many lenders who supported our project and whom we would like to thank first. In addition to many private individuals who agreed to part with their treasures for several months, we are also indebted to the company collections of BMW Group Classic, Daimler AG, Archiv und Fahrzeugsammlung Mercedes-Benz Classic, Toyota Deutschland GmbH, and Autostadt GmbH in Wolfsburg, whose precious loans also contribute to the success of this project.

I would furthermore like to thank all my colleagues at the Kunstpalast. Such a project is always the product of teamwork and can only be made a reality collaboratively, and with a great deal of professional commitment. We would like to thank Liman Design for the design, and Hirmer Verlag for producing the exhibition catalogue. We owe the captivating catalogue contributions to the authors Christopher Butt, Markus Caspers, Dieter Castenow, Niklas Maak, Barbara Til and Paolo Tumminelli. The essays reveals not just the authors' great knowledge, but also their passion for the subject.

The exhibition was successfully accompanied at every level and with great commitment by project leader Bianca Raitz, to whom I would also like to extend my gratitude. Finally, my greatest thanks go to the two curators, Barbara Til and Dieter Castenow. Together they did not just bring about this wonderful and highly ambitious project; they also guided it across the finish line with great passion and intuition, and at just the right speed.

Felix Krämer
Director, Kunstpalast

Giulietta speciale
BERTONE
ALFA ROMEO
MILANO

SCULPTURAL AND TIMELESS BEAUTY: SPORTS CARS BETWEEN CULT AND CULTURE

BARBARA TIL,
DIETER CASTENOW

Visitors from another planet would not have to search for long to find an engineered object of unique cultural value, one which embodies the spirit of our age through cultural and aesthetic forms of expression. In fact, such a revealing artefact has been racing through our solar system since February 2018: a metallic-red roadster made by Tesla, the American manufacturer of electric vehicles. Behind the wheel, a dummy in a space suit, correctly buckled in, who goes by the name of Starman – a nod to David Bowie! En route to Mars, the sports car is travelling at thousands of kilometres per hour on its orbit around the sun – but certainly not thanks to its electric motor. Instead, the cabriolet was catapulted into orbit from Cape Canaveral at the top of a launch vehicle owned by the private Californian company Space X during an initial test flight.[1] [Fig. 1] It was a great media coup for Elon Musk, the founder of Tesla and Space X – on the day, 2.3 million viewers watched the YouTube livestream. This publicity stunt also demonstrates the significance and desires we continue to project onto automobiles.

Even people who have a more dismissive attitude to automobiles discover that a car is never just a car; rather, it is always a medium for aesthetics, prestige, emotion, passion, social distinction, and status-giving charisma. It is an adornment, an accessory, a prop, a tool for self-presentation, a refuge, a weapon, a lover, a companion, in short 'a semantically highly variable socio-cultural figuration'.[2]

However, why does an object whose original purpose was to increase individual mobility keep reinventing itself, not just as a piece of engineering but first and foremost as an aesthetic artefact? And why do so many people still see it as a cult object and symbol of individual freedom, even though it has actually long surpassed its functional purpose? The answer is as multifaceted as the one-hundred-and-thirty-year history of the automobile itself. The stories of the designers and engineers behind the development of the automobile were not important for its success – hardly anyone has heard of Franco Scaglione, Malcolm Sayer, Paul Bracq or Albrecht von Goertz. Rather, it is a mythically charged narrative in which design, technology, symbolism and mobility are presented as having heroic, divine and near magical connotations. And this view has not been put forward solely by the Futurists, but also by many other artists, musicians, film-makers and writers of both sexes, even today. In 1922 Claire Goll wrote in *Zwanzigstes Jahrhundert*: 'O cosmic feeling of speed! / You, my century! / Electrically powered, racing drivers against the sun, headlights against the stars / I'm yours!'[3] Thirty years later, Roland Barthes moved the Citroën DS into celestial spheres

Fig. 1: The Tesla Roadster has been floating through space with a dummy behind the wheel since February 2018

by praising it as a 'cosmic being' and, from the fact that 'DS' and the French word 'déesse' (goddess) sound the same, said the car was a divine apparition, a 'magical' and a 'superlative *object*', which 'obviously' appeared to have 'fallen from sky'. Whether proverbially fallen from heaven or not, the presentation of the DS at the Paris Motor Show in 1962[4] as a futuristic object, a metaphorical, sculptural phenomenon, once again heightened the sense that this was an object that could have been created only by an artist, albeit an unknown one.[5] [Fig. 2] Like the medieval masters who built the Gothic cathedrals, whose working methods in the stonemasons' lodges were similar to those employed in the *carrozzerias* in Italy during the 1950s and early 1960s, both focusing on work executed by the hands of a craftsman in a protected workshop. This was possible in sports-car manufacturing since the vehicles were often produced in small, select production runs, or even as one-of-a-kind cars. There were even designers and coachbuilders who created models by hand, without drawings or plans, such as Sergio Scaglietti, whose company worked closely with Ferrari.

This approach is based on a deeply rooted desire for sublime and iconic beauty and strength, which tellingly found its fulfilment in the twentieth century and specifically in the bright opportunities presented by the automobile, in the pleasurable promise of speed, beauty and emotion. Sports cars and racing cars meet this intense emotional need most keenly since nowhere else is the mythical narrative of 'petrol in the blood', of the thrill of speed, a lust for adventure and for experiencing one's limits, celebrated as openly as in racing, which thereby deepens the symbolic charge of the automobile. Until World War Two, it was racing cars that caused a sensation; after that it was sports cars, the domesticated version of their racing cousins.

A further important factor has to be considered: a sports car, be it a cabriolet or a coupé, is never perceived as a utility object in the conventional sense. Instead, it is seen as an expression of aesthetics, style and passion, in short as a product of the avant-garde. This cultural codification meant that from the beginning sports cars acted as vehicles for certain desires and dreams, making them both artworks and objects that stimulate our imagination.

MODELLED SURFACE – KINETIC GADGET

The decades from the 1950s to the 1970s were among the most outstanding for sports-car design. Over the course of these decades, young designers, coachbuilders and engineers developed coupés and cabriolets of incredible elegance, ingenuity and intensity. The Golden Ratio was often used as the design principle. This was the case for example with the Porsche 356 and 911 [Fig. 3] and with the wonderfully harmonious proportions of the sports cars designed by Battista 'Pinin' Farina. As a result, a level of design was achieved that went far beyond just skilled manual work and that incorporated the flowing transitions from craftsmanship to art. This is already reflected in 1946 in 'Pinin' Farina's Cisitalia sports car – it features the iconic combination of classic and new proportions: flat, flowing, horizontal. In addition to the dynamically elongated body, it is the innovative shaping of the front of the vehicle in particular that almost follows facial proportions: the headlights are integrated into the front grille and the car is given a 'face' with googly eyes, somewhat emulating childlike features with a friendly gaze. [Fig. 4] It is a design whose amorphous lines exude harmony and elegance and whose characteristics can be found in a large number of sports cars of the 1950s (see pp. 37, 41, 53, 57).

During the following decade, the aesthetic changed radically and lastingly: from the end of the 1960s, the front of the car becomes flat and stretched out and merges with the windscreen without transition. The grille and its emblematic significance for a vehicle's design and make fades away, as do the headlights that now blend with the bonnet, causing the sports car to look eyeless. As a result, the entire visual weight is put on the rear. This profound change in vehicle design, which began with the Lamborghini Miura (see p. 108), also gives us an insight into the aesthetic, symbolic and sociological interpretation of certain autobody shapes – in this case, the 'wedge' shape. With the disappearance of the curvy, organic and streamlined design in favour of an angular, flat aesthetic, a formal language with dynamic, aggressive and masculine connotations takes centre stage in the late 1960s and transforms the sports car into a martial, kinetic object. However, all this is done with a twinkle in the eye, for the cars' mostly bright colours give them a toy-like, cheerful character.

COLOUR CHOICE – COLOUR MAKES THE CAR

Black and grey are always possible – as a glance at the dull sight presented by today's streets shows – and the same is true for sports cars. However, a car's colour plays a crucial role for both aesthetic and psychological reasons. Trying to determine the character of the person behind the wheel through the colour of the vehicle is a popular pastime. Those who opt for red, for example, are considered impulsive and outgoing, or safety fanatics; a silver or grey colour suggests understatement, while drivers of black cars are considered authoritarian, self-confident and ambitious. However, colour is also a crucial factor in the coherence of a vehicle's design and formal quality, emphasising both emotional and functional elements. Cars in light colours – and this is particularly true for sports cars – seem wider, softer and lighter, while dark colours suggest the vehicle is hard, heavy and high quality. In addition, some colour designs have over time developed into veritable codes. Ferrari red, for example, stands for the dynamism of a very particular shade of red that became synonymous with

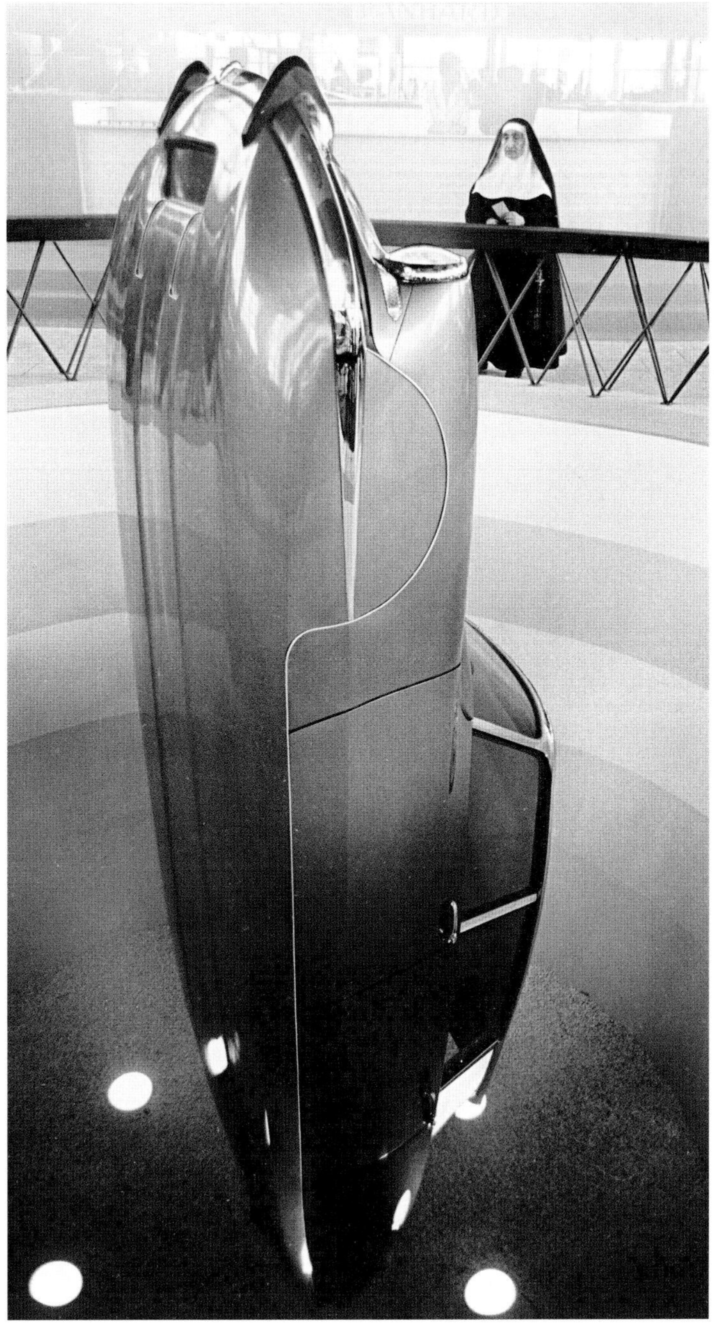

Fig. 2: Citroën DS, Flaminio Bertoni, 1955, Paris Motor Show 1962

Fig. 3: Rear view of the Porsche 911s of 1963 and 2011 with the Golden Ratio shown
Fig. 4: Alfa Romeo Giulietta Sprint Speciale (SS), Prototipo, Franco Scaglione, 1957

the racing cars and later also for the sports cars produced by Ferrari. The classic red of the Alfa Romeo is also embedded in a colour context that puts the past, present and future of the company into tension with each other. The meanings we give to colours reveal similarities to associations in language. Just as we learn a language, so our understanding of colours is shaped by experience. When it comes to the Mercedes-Benz 300 SL, silver is steadfastly associated with the German racing cars the Silver Arrows, which have enjoyed a legendary reputation since the 1930s. This status lived on in the colour and design of production coupés, which is proved by – among other things – the sales figures at the time: 526 silver versions were produced, but only 15 of the Bordeaux red 300 SL. This difference becomes apparent when presenting two otherwise identical 300 SL models, one silver, one red, next to each other. It becomes obvious how colour serves as a meta-level for cultural and aesthetic values. [Fig. 5]

Until the 1970s, it was still easy to discern social and engineering changes based on colour trends: fashion, furniture, mobility – everything was presented in similar shades. During the 1950s, after the black and white of the war years, cars came in light, optimistic colours: a Celeste (sky blue) for the Alfa Giulietta Spider, light grey for Porsche and a respectable egg shell for BMW. The loud, garish colours of the late 1960s and 1970s stand for a real zest for life and for the urge for individuality – a period steeped in orange, lime green, sunshine yellow and bright red.

Colours are more diverse today. We no longer have colours that are in fashion and that permeate almost every area of life, so it seems that conformity is the order of the day when it comes to cars right now. And this is also reflected in their design.

SPEED OF LIFE – THE AESTHETICS OF SPEED

To begin with, speed is an abstract quantity – modes of transport and modern information technologies have made this dynamic force something we can see and experience. With the advent of the automobile in the early twentieth century, speed was celebrated as a mark of modernity. The sports car in particular is built to give people a way to experience the pleasure of speed. Its vitality is the paradigmatic embodiment of mobility.[6] When an engine becomes loud and starts vibrating at high revs, the concurrence of the ecstasy of speed and the pleasure of acceleration produces an intense feeling. Pure adventure, life is experienced as a strong shot of adrenaline; at the same time, it feels like escape, a scenario in which the sports car becomes the getaway vehicle. The thrill of speed promises an intense and immediate life, coupled with the longing for absolute freedom. No fear of death! Quite the contrary, a real sports-car driver savours this euphoric feeling of going to the limit and sometimes even a little bit beyond. 'Angstlust'[7] – 'desire for fear', i.e. the exhilarating feeling after a near-miss, which therefore importantly was a miss – is a mixture of adrenaline and a thrill that keeps demanding more and even riskier recklessness. In this context, Peter Sloterdijk refers to our 'archaic

Fig. 5: Mercedes-Benz 300 SL Coupé (silver and bordeaux), Friedrich Geiger, Karl Wilfert, 1955 and 1957

Fig. 6: Claude Lelouch, *C'était un rendez-vous*, 1976, film still

willingness to pay a price in blood'.[8] According to Paul Virilio, objects rushing past us at high speed form a paradigm, at least visually, for the 'dissolution of matter in dromoscopic intoxication in which the windows of the vehicle turn into screens on to which the objects are projected'.[9]

Claude Lelouch's portrayal, in the 1976 film *C'était un rendez-vous*, of a breakneck drive in a sports car through Paris early in the morning recorded from the cockpit view of the driver summarises this experience of our limits in a nutshell: the racing Ferrari 275 GTB/4 (see p. 103) becomes a *projector projectile* that removes the materiality of objects.[10] [Fig. 6]

… IN THE MIDST OF SOCIETY

Cars are without doubt a reflection of the socio-cultural dynamic in our society. And even though their practical utility has been questioned more and more in recent decades, there is almost no object that has been created in a more sophisticated, imaginative manner and that is a greater projection screen than the automobile.

The exhibition presents 29 high-quality, outstanding sports cars, decontextualised from their function, and portrays their significance as 'automobile design objects' by focusing on their sculptural and synaesthetic properties. Using a number of themes such as racing, prototypes and luxury vehicles, the exhibition zeroes in on the significance of sports cars and the development of their design between the 1950s and the 1960s. During this period, coachbuilders and designers – especially Italian ones – produced fascinating highlights in automobile design; they include Battista 'Pinin' Farina with the sought-after Lancia and Alfa Romeo sports cars, Nuccio Bertone among others with his aerodynamic, elegant Alfa Romeo Giulietta SS, and Marcello Gandini with his veritably prototypical Lamborghinis. However, the designers at BMW, Mercedes-Benz and Porsche also created vehicles that set international standards and that became 'dream cars' for eternity, such as the Mercedes 300 SL gullwing. The British meanwhile, with their sense of tradition, produced a real fixed star in the automobile heavens with their 'cool and charming' Jaguar E-type. Beyond that there are also some unknown models waiting to be discovered: the Bizzarrini GT Strada 5300, the exclusive French Facel Vega, and the unique sports car from the far east, the Toyota 2000 GT, which in its day could have given a Ferrari a run for its money.

SYNAESTHETIC SCULPTURE – LUXURY PRODUCT

The artistic and emotional charge embodied in a sports car – a charge unabated to this day – undoubtedly makes it a medium of the avant-garde and at the same time a high-quality product of the market. It is not least the immense increase in value experienced by historical automobiles, particularly the sports cars of the 1940s and 1950s, that makes them seem like works of art to us. Luxurious trade fairs and auctions in acclaimed institutions of the art trade have long presented vintage cars alongside the visual arts as investments that hold their value for their high-end clientele. An exhibition in a public museum such as *CARS* that focuses on the sculptural, aesthetic dimension of the sports car raises the standing of the exhibits even further. It is of course possible to be critical of this development. But at the same time, we must ask ourselves why historic cars have achieved such an 'aura'. It is not enough to argue merely about appeal, demand and the mechanisms of the market. What makes these vehicles special is based on a paradoxical construct of desires, projections and aesthetic symbols, and is less about engineering or the history of progress than we might believe. That which we call progress is relative to the ever-changing social, cultural and political significance that society gives to cars. 'The history of progress of the automobile is a cultural narrative itself, aimed at characterising certain technical parameters compared to other attributes.'[11] This means that in addition to the material culture, social and aesthetic parameters play crucial roles in taking the sports car into the realm of the sculptural and transforming it into a complete synaesthetic experience of touch, smell, sound and, in relation to their colour, vision. It is in this experience which reveals our fascination with the merging of form, engineering, perfection and the human driver or passenger, as well as our fascination with destruction and death – but also our passion and our lust for life.

1 See The New York Times, 6 February 2018, online at: https://www.nytimes.com/2018/02/06/science/falcon-heavy-spacex-launch.html (accessed July 2018).
2 Roland Wetzel (ed.), Fetisch Auto. Ich fahre, also bin ich, exh. cat. Museum Tinguely Basel, Heidelberg/Berlin 2011, p. 57.
3 Quoted from: Johannes Bilstein (ed.), Ich bin mein Auto. Die maschinalen Ebenbilder des Menschen, exh. cat. Staatliche Kunsthalle Baden-Baden, Cologne 2001, p. 163.
4 The Citroën 19 DS was first shown at the Paris Motor Show in 1955.
5 See Roland Barthes, The New Citroën, in: Mythologies (1957), London 1964, pp. 88–89.
6 See Filippo Tommaso Marinetti, Manifesto del Futurismo (1909), trans. as Manifesto of Futurism, in: Umbro Apollonio (ed.), Documents of 20th Century Art, New York 1973, pp. 19-24; online at: http://viola.informatik.uni-bremen.de/typo/fileadmin/media/lernen/Futurist_Manifesto.pdf (accessed July 2018).
7 Exh. cat. Basel 2011 (as note 2), p. 236.
8 Peter Sloterdijk, Die Gesellschaft der Kentauren. Philosophische Bemerkungen der Automobilität, in: Frankfurter Allgemeine Zeitung Magazin, 634, 24 April 1992, p. 36.
9 See Paul Virilio, Rasender Stillstand, Munich 1992, p. 29. English edition: Polar Inertia, trans. Patrick Camiller, London 2000.
10 Ibid., p. 29. For the drive, Lelouch used a Mercedes 450 SEL 6.9, as the Ferrari vibrated too strongly. The engine sound was that of the Ferrari 275 GTB/4.
11 Exh. cat. Basel 2011 (as note 2), p. 57.

IN PRAISE OF THE SPORTS CAR

NIKLAS MAAK

ENCOUNTER WITH A SPIRIT

Even people who are not interested in cars should look at them. There is no other branch of the economy where so much money is invested in aesthetic seduction, in appeals to our subconscious, in psychological warfare as in automobile construction; and in no other industry is as much money earned with them. As recently as the 1950s, the majority of the West German budget was spent on food; today, housing and transport have pushed it to third place. Automobile manufacturers spend billions on the design and marketing of new models – and maybe that is why the aesthetic and psychosocial trends of a society are reflected more precisely in automobile design than in any other area.

At the start of this development was the *Spirit of Ecstasy* of 1911, a bonnet ornament designed by sculptor Charles Sykes that Rolls-Royce, a make then known for sporting high-performance cars, fitted to its vehicles. [Fig. 1] It was part of one of the first meticulously planned image campaigns of the automobile industry. Even the name of the sculpture carried a promise of happiness made by the auto industry that continues to enthral us to the present day – departure, freedom, flight, a life of speed.

The small figurine reactivated a forgotten, ambivalent image of speed that was first created during the Renaissance: it is the tempting, but also dangerous speed, *Velocitas*, that Cesare Ripa depicted in his compendium of personifications, *Iconologia*: unlike *Celeritas* and *Agilitas*, it does not represent an orderly pace, but acceleration, an abandonment of inhibitions, racing, mania and delirium. [Fig. 2] This ancient image of the ecstasy of acceleration returns with the *Spirit of Ecstasy*, now in a positive light, as a promise of an uninhibited, fast-paced life. It is the first and most effective representation of the dream of a life in the fast lane without which the unabated fascination with driving in general, and with sports cars in particular, would be unthinkable.

LIFE IN THE FAST LANE: THE EARLY HISTORY OF THE SPORTS CAR

The love of sports cars is older than the automobile. As far back as the sixteenth century, the experience of fast, comfortable travel was seen as a pleasure. The Swiss cultural historian Jacob Burckhardt stated that 'In the well-paved streets of Italian cities, driving was universal, while elsewhere in Europe walking or riding was the custom, and at all events no one drove for amusement',[1] while Matteo Bandello and Ariosto remarked on the emerging culture surrounding driving and vehicles in Italian

Fig. 1: Rolls-Royce bonnet ornament: *Spirit of Ecstasy*, designed in 1911 by Charles Sykes

cities in which richly gilded and carved carriages drawn by two or four horses became fashionable.[2]

According to the Duke of Saint-Simon in his memoirs, the French king Louis XIV had his carriages lowered so that they would not topple over when going fast. He was in the habit of 'travelling at an exceptional speed. Those who became sick in the process quickly lost the King's favour'.[3] Louis XIV drove quickly but was no racer – but even they existed in his day. The deplorable custom of racing in the narrow streets of the centre of Paris claimed so many victims in the 16th century that Francis I found it necessary in 1539 to impose the first speed limit in history.[4]

When the automobile came along a few centuries later, making speeds of more than 100 kilometres per hour a reality, there was no stopping people. On the country roads of Barbizon south of Paris, previously a location for painting contemplative forest scenes, individuals like Max Ernst, André Derain and Louis Aragon met in borrowed sports cars 'pour faire de la vitesse' – 'to make speed'. The collective disinhibition scandals of bohemians no longer took place in the studio but on the streets – and the pedestrians who had to leap aside when the artists came rattling along were outraged.

Anyone reading reports from the early days of the motor car must conclude that it was invented only in order to indulge in a new physical pleasure: automobile racing. It is one of the most stubborn myths in automobile history that right from the start visionary benefactors had nothing but mass car ownership and the construction of ambulances in mind. In reality, the pioneer car manufacturers wanted pure speed. Car inventors like Albert de Dion described how much they liked racing through the Bois de Boulogne, watching how the startled horses reared up and threw off their aristocratic riders. Early cars were no aids to society, they were the expression of a new speed-focused dandyism: if the older generation of dandies strolled along with a tortoise on a leash, removing themselves from the social pressure for speed by radically slowing down, the new dandy did so by pointlessly increasing it. Too feeble and vulnerable for actual transportation, the first cars were pure ecstasy machines. In his famous *Manifesto of Futurism* of 1909, Filippo Marinetti wrote: 'We declare that the splendor of the world has been enriched by a new beauty: the beauty of speed. A racing automobile with its bonnet adorned with great tubes like serpents with explosive breath [...] a roaring motor car which seems to run on machine-gun fire, is more beautiful than the Winged Victory of Samothrace.'[5] [Fig. 3]

Drivers in the early days of the automobile experienced an anti-social high that culminated in Marinetti's gleeful remark that they would race on 'crushing beneath our burning

Fig. 2: Cesare Ripa, *Velocitas*, Venice, 1645

wheels, like shirt-collars under the iron, the watch dogs on the steps of the houses'.[6] The driver who, as Marinetti exulted, became a modern centaur in his vehicle, felt like a superhuman hero who did battle with the elements and with gravity and emerged victorious: even around 1895 it was possible to achieve acceleration forces in cars that no horse-drawn carriage could equal. Passengers noted with irritation that their hats would fly off – 'and, strangely, forwards' – when their chauffeur put his foot down. The racing of the early years was all the more sinister to health officials and officers of the law as it displayed clear traits of sexual ecstasy. In Germany in 1904, Doctor Paul Näcke published an essay titled 'Der Geisteszustand des Automobilfahrers' (The State of Mind of the Automobile Driver) in which he issued a warning that driving produced 'misanthropic behaviour'; the person behind the wheel felt a 'kind of fogginess of the senses' when racing along in a vehicle, which tempted him to ever faster and daring driving manoeuvres.[7]

When Lena Amsel, the lover of Max Ernst, Louis Aragon and André Derain, died during an illegal race in her Bugatti in 1929, the press turned it into one of the biggest artist scandals of the day. A furious death at high speed soon became a part of modern legends as the only appropriate end for an exquisite, suicidal lifestyle: the dancer Isadora Duncan died in Nice in 1927 when her scarf became tangled up in the spokes of an accelerating Amilcar and she was flung out of the vehicle, her neck broken; in 1935, Prince Alexis Mdivani, husband of American heiress Barbara Woolworth Hutton, ploughed his Rolls-Royce into a tree

Fig. 3: Porfirio Rubirosa and Odile Rodin in a Mercedes-Benz 300 SL, 1950s

Fig. 4: Dustin Hoffman as Benjamin Braddock in the Alfa Romeo Spider in *The Graduate*, directed by Mike Nichols, 1967

during an attempt to overtake the fast train between Paris and Madrid; the playboy Porfirio Rubirosa died when he smashed his Ferrari into a tree in the Bois de Boulogne after an all-night celebration in 1965; and James Dean's premature end turned the actor into a legend.

RACING AND TRAVELLING: SPORTS CARS VS. THE GRAN TURISMO

We have to be precise: not every fast car is a sports car. Sports cars never have cup holders and they are never automatic. They are controlled by hand; it is the gear stick that produces the direct element, the immediate communication, the merging of body and machine, the intensity of the driving experience: sports cars – especially the open roadsters and convertibles – have always also been machines with which to experience the elements, the wind, sun and speed, the natural forces of nature, more intensely. The goal of the sports car is not to transport individuals from A to B; it is to intensify sensations and the enjoyment of acceleration and G-forces.

The sports car must be distinguished from the Gran Turismo. GTs are fast, two-door vehicles with two seats (and only occasionally a dickey or a child's seat) as well as a boot in which to stow luggage for a long weekend by the sea or in the mountains. Every feature of a GT is aimed at getting passengers from their location to a more beautiful location both quickly and in style. While drivers of a sports car find happiness on a race track, which will always take them back to their starting point, GT drivers want to escape to a warmer, more beautiful world: driving a sports car is circular, driving a GT is linear. The first car races went from Paris to the South; the British gentry charged from their rainy homes to the warmth of the Mediterranean; the round racetrack therefore has an air of melancholy abstraction, of idling.

Sports cars are fetish objects, too loud, too low and too hot for everyday use; they mainly serve the desire for pure acceleration. GTs are escape vehicles. They are about both going fast and travelling.

Both vehicles types are available with or without a roof. The cabriolet is older than the car. In the days before the combustion engine, people went on trips in open carriages drawn by two horses. The name comes from the French word *cabrioler*, which means something like 'to caper' or 'to leap'. This demonstrates the central significance of the sports car, with or without an engine, with or without a roof: it is not there for transportation, it is there for pleasure. It is the vehicle for a wilder, wind-blown life. [Fig. 4]

Ever since the stars and playboys of the 1960s, from Porfirio Rubirosa to Steve McQueen and Alain Delon, were seen in open Ferraris, since Brigitte Bardot travelled to Saint-Tropez in her Renault Floride, Dustin Hoffman rushed to his girlfriend in his Alfa Romeo Spider, and the Roman *alta borghesia* sped to Orbetello in their open Maserati Ghiblis, the cabriolet has been seen as the highest form of motorised fulfilment. At a time when cars became increasingly comfortable and quiet and were fitted with better air suspension, the open sports car brought back the experience of wind, heat and speed that had become locked away behind double glazing and air-conditioning units in everyday life: it was a machine to intensify our experience of the world.

Drivers of open sports cars state that they expect speed, wind, sonorous noise and burning heat from life and that it is the search for adventure and intensity that determines the choice of things they surround themselves with, not the fear of death; these drivers live without roll bars.

We can speculate on what it means that the stars of today are no longer driving cabriolets but four-by-fours. Streets are no longer a location for self-presentation; they have become combat zones that vehicles traverse with blacked-out windows: even the cars wear sunglasses.

The SUV, stuffed to the brim with leather seats, air-conditioning, wooden veneer and on-board entertainment systems, blanks out the outside world. The temperature inside is constant, whether there is tarmac, snow or sand under the wheels. The SUV takes real estate on the road: the living room is everywhere, summer is indicated only by a matt glimmer behind tinted windows. The overriding motivation behind the design is to protect passengers from danger. As is the case with many things these days, the SUV is designed with death in mind: its formal language does not say happiness, it says there is a danger of crashing, of failing, of encountering the worst-case scenario.

The open sports car is the opposite: lighter, more open, a machine that makes the experience of speed and the environment, the wind and the sun, more intense; it does not hide these features. A car like the Ferrari California Spyder, in which Alain Delon showed himself with Jane Fonda [Fig. p. 68], does not portray an image of potential dangers but of the joys of acceleration, the burning sun, the sonorous roaring of the engine in a tunnel on the Côte d'Azur, of life in the best-case scenario.

Fig. 5: Lamborghini Miura S Serie II, Marcello Gandini, 1970

THE ORGANIC AND THE GEOMETRIC: THE TWO BODIES OF THE SPORTS CAR

The first sports cars still resembled carriages in appearance. It was merely the length of the bonnet that gave away the forces the driver would experience behind the wheel of such a fast car. It was not long, however, before coachbuilders and designers tried to express the experience of acceleration these vehicles made possible through the shape they gave them; and when the streamlined form emerged in the 1950s, the motorised carriage was transformed into a structure with human-like characteristics – it was given chrome breasts and metal hips and thereby became the illusion of the perfect technoid body. When Citroën named its revolutionary limousine featuring hydropneumatic suspension 'DS' – pronounced 'dé-esse' (goddess) – in 1955, it became obvious that the engineered object was also seen, metaphorically, as the ideal body.

The period from the 1950s to the 1970s could be seen as the High Renaissance of automobile construction. This period was the last in which designers could still work on spectacular forms while being largely unencumbered by concerns about market research, cost-effectiveness or safety requirements. Those fond of classical proportions will not tire from

Fig. 6: Lamborghini Countach LP400, 1974

emphasising that the designers who worked at Pininfarina during these decades based the proportions of their vehicles on the principle of the Golden Ratio – the principle that characterises the forms of the Renaissance villas by Raphael, da Sangallo and Palladio. The ratio between the length of the vehicle and its greenhouse, between the height of the wheel arches and the height of the overall vehicle, between the placement of the power dome – all these have been calculated using the Golden Ratio, with small irregularities and dramatisations intended as accents that bring a level of dynamism to the overall appearance without undermining it.

However, even back then one sports-car company stood out because it cared more about the radical dramatisation of the autobody than about giving the impression of dynamic harmony. It belonged to a man whose name was for a long time associated with trundling tractors and humming fridges, with rural Italy where nothing shimmered in metallic gold, where nothing roared with twelve cylinders. It was in that location, in the flat plains around Bologna, that Ferruccio Lamborghini, the son of a simple farmer, was born on 28 April 1916, under the sign of Taurus. After 1945, he bought up all the junk the war had left behind – old Italian tanks and German lorries – and welded and riveted them for a long time until they bore a convincing resemblance to tractors. The farmers loved Lamborghini for this and he became rich as a tractor maker. He also built helicopters and air-conditioning units – but his name became truly glamorous only when he finally decided to challenge the king of carmakers, Ferrari, to a duel. The first Lamborghini 350 GTV was produced in 1964, and in 1966 the Miura was added – just seven years before the Oil Crisis that deflated the sports-car business for a while. The Miura was, nevertheless, the climax and consummation of an era. Powered by a transversely mounted V12 mid-engine, it had a radical chic that could not be purchased anywhere else. It was hysterically flat, even compared to a Ferrari, hysterically fast, and as far removed from all sense of moderation as possible. In contrast to the Ferraris with their Apollonian beauty, the Miura was anything but classical and restrained – Ferrari is to Lamborghini what the Renaissance is to Mannerism. Lamborghinis were loud, radical, exhibitionist and closer to monsters than the gods (the Miura was somehow reminiscent of a deep-sea fish). [Fig. 5] Just five years later another Lamborghini put an end to an entire era: Lamborghini called it 'Countach', a name for which there are several explanations – for instance, that it is a word from the piedmont dialect, an exclamation of great surprise that could be translated as 'unsurpassable!'. [Fig. 6]

The Countach was presented as a concept car in Geneva in March 1971, with a longitudinally mounted twelve-cylinder engine in the rear, a tubular frame, a five-speed gearbox located in front of the engine and a driveshaft that ran through the sump to the differential. In addition, it had scissor doors that opened upwards and tilted forwards in a semi-circular manner. However, the autobody was a shock: nothing was round. The Countach demonstrated like almost no other production vehicle the transition in sports-car design from the organic and the anthropomorphic to the geometric – from body to structure. Almost every aspect of the Countach bar the tyres and the steering wheel was geometric, rectangular and linear.

Other sports-car manufacturers had also been preparing to take this step, but only in concept cars – Alfa Romeo for example: a comparison between the rounded Giulia Sprint GTA [Fig. 7] with its pleasant headlights, and the Alfa Romeo Carabo's bright green, wedge shaped, eyeless vehicle with yellow lips, brown polished glass windows and black plastic slats, which already heralded the new style of the 1970s, demonstrates just how big the design leap was that the company took between 1966 and 1969, the year of the lunar landing. The Alfa Carabo, designed by Bertone, which highlights the transition from a modernity of metal and glass to the plastic age, looks like it was flung into the present from outer space. [Fig. p. 154] Next to it and the Countach, the curvaceous metal bodies of the automobile High Renaissance suddenly looked like antiques.

Both have earned their place in the museum. As is the case of all great artworks, they reveal in their shapes the hopes and fears, the moods and obsessions, of their day more clearly than almost every other cultural product.

Fig. 7: Alfa Romeo Giulia Sprint GTA, Autodelta, 1965

FULL SPEED AHEAD FOR ALL: PORSCHE, ALFA ROMEO AND THE DEMOCRATISATION OF THE SPORTS CAR

Automobile design reveals a lot about the state of a society. Makes such as Alfa Romeo in particular are interesting to sociologists, too: the company from Milan served an elite market of top earners prior to World War Two and was also mainly successful with racing cars (in 1925 Alfa Romeo won the first Grand Prix season, the Automobile World Championship). The Alfa Romeo 2900 models from the 1930s did not just have the most beautiful teardrop rears in Italian design history, created by coachbuilders such as Zagato, Touring, Castagna, Pininfarina or Figoni, depending on customer wishes; they were not just the fastest production vehicles in the world with a top speed of 205 kilometres per hour – they were also extremely expensive and exclusive. However, after World War Two the company suddenly began targeting a broader, middle-class audience – the Giuliettas, the Giulias, and the Spider that Dustin Hoffman drove through California in the 1967 film *The Graduate*, making it famous around the world, were the main vehicles that illustrate this fundamental shift. They made the speeds and the roaring, smoky, dusty summer sound, the dark timbre of the Alfa engines that escapes no VW, and that is caused by the combination of the two chain-driven overhead camshafts

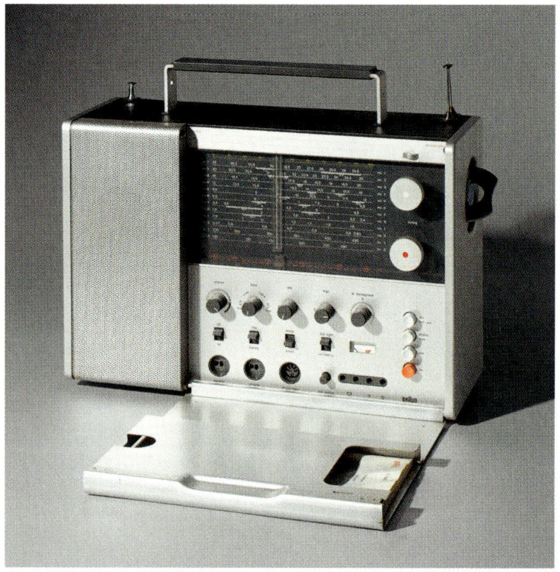

Fig. 8: Braun short-wave radio receiver T 1000 in aluminium, designer Dieter Rams, 1963

and the two twin carburettors, affordable for the masses.

Just like that of Alfa Romeo, Porsche's success is also associated with the development of the somewhat levelled middle-class society after 1945. Anyone who drove a Lamborghini or a Corvette was considered neurotic about their image, arrogant, criminal or just downright embarrassing, particularly in the strongholds of middle-class society; they annoyed people because they so very clearly did not want anything to do with them.

In comparison, a Porsche was always a socially acceptable form of luxury. Designed by Ferdinand Porsche and Erwin Komenda, the inventor of the Volkswagen after World War Two, the first Porsche was nothing but a flattened somewhat faster Beetle, small and with googly eyes – the exact opposite of an unattainable sports car. The former shot-putter and doctor Hedda Heuser, who was one of the first women to enter the Bundestag for the FDP, proudly posed in front of her Porsche for a magazine in the early 1960s. Voters evidently did not object to this. The car looked safe and friendly enough to avoid seeming immoral.

Ulf Poschardt, who wrote the most intelligent and knowledgeable book on the 911, sees in the first Porsche of the post-war period the aesthetic antithesis to 'the powerful compressor Mercedes of the Nazis that seemed to have come from Arno Breker's studio'. [Fig. p. 95] The Porsche 356 was the exact opposite and therefore also a symbol of the new Germany after 1945: modest, small, and with a friendly way of making eyes.

In 1963 its successor, the Porsche 911 – which was called the 901 at the time, but this was changed at the insistence of Peugeot, who had legally reserved the right to the number 901 – combined this subtle, agreeable sports-car aesthetic with its Bauhaus ethics. It was smoother and longer, and with its large glassed areas much lighter than its Beetle-like predecessor. It was introduced in the same year in which the legendary designer Dieter Rams presented his Braun shortwave radio receiver T 1000 [Fig. 8] and Mies van der Rohe presented his design for the Neue Nationalgalerie in Berlin [Fig. 9].

What connected all three designs was their strict, technically reticent lines. Their forms were forward-looking. They were not to stir up memories of anything, like containers waiting to be filled; they pointed to the future. Not the object itself but the result that it made possible was to be the focus of attention: music that could be taken anywhere; the exhibited objects, unmolested by a strong architectural decorum; the experience of speed and passion that was not to be hampered by a homey, cosy interior. It is no surprise that many architects loved the Porsche 911: like the buildings of the International Style, it exhibited a design that housed the engine, seats and trunk space in a highly efficient form and that eschewed ornament. There were no shark fins, no decorative metal curves, no temple-like chrome radiator grille – the 911 was a car without bay and dormer windows, as it were. These days it is seen as *the* classic in German automobile design, a masterpiece of engineering that discards everything superfluous.

But none of this should deceive us: the Porsche 911 featured a racy wholly un-Germanic hedonism that other classics of the often somewhat dry Bauhaus beauty did not have: the 911's greenhouse, the driver's cabin and its tapered elliptical side window, exhibits such verve that we could be forgiven for thinking the designer's pen itself wanted to get on to the racetrack – without ever crossing the line between being dynamic and over-revving, the disintegration of form. Considered from the perspective of formal aesthetics, a Porsche is always a complex entity, the tension lying in increasing the intensity between contrasting elements: what we see is a gracefully built, almost narrow entity on the one hand, but a well-toned, muscular one on the other. At the rear, between the slightly widening hips of the fender, where the engine – the vehicle's power centre – is located, the lines are concentrated as if under high voltage. At the front, on the other hand, the calm of a wide, empty space between headlights set far apart dominates. Satori, the Asian art of emptiness, at the front, rock 'n' roll at the back: the design expresses the constructive idiosyncrasy of a rear-engine vehicle.

GTO INSTEAD OF GRANADA: THE SOCIOLOGY OF NAMES

Sports cars are engineering artworks. While the bourgeoisie sitting in sedans with velour seats dream of aristocratic titles ('Comtesse'), faraway destinations ('Granada', 'Eldorado Biarritz') or esteemed job titles ('Kapitän' = 'captain'; 'Diplomat'), sports-car drivers are characterised by the ideal of the alert engine operator, and by the cold metallic atmosphere of their acceleration devices. The technophile cult is also reflected in the unsentimental terminology given to the models of famous sports cars: 911, 250 GT, 275 GT, E-type, B24, 2000 GT, DB4, 5000. At best they occasionally get a suffix such as 'California', 'Mexico' or 'Carrera', not in order to encourage customers to dream, but because a famous race had been won in those locations. And technophile model names are not always attractive: German cars, especially premium vehicles, go overboard in their unemotional image: Audis sound like paper formats (A4, A5), AMG Mercedes sedans like minor roads (E63), BMWs like a clause in a German statute book addressing an exception to a contract that has not been fulfilled (320).

Fig. 9: Neue Nationalgalerie (model 34.5 x 217 x 166.7 cm), Ludwig Mies van der Rohe, Berlin, 1965–1968, Kunstbibliothek, Staatliche Museen zu Berlin

Car names are somewhat matter-of-fact in Italy, too. Cars there have been given names such as 'Maserati / Quattroporte / Ottocilindri / Evolutione', which sounds lovely in Italian but means nothing more than 'Maserati / four-door / eight-cylinder / updated model'. Then there is the Alfa Romeo Giulia Quadrifoglio. These are not just car names, they are onomatopoeic promises: if you utter these names loudly and quickly enough, they sound like the cars themselves, which, if you switch from third to second gear in a sharp hairpin bend somewhere outside Fiesole, sound as if the engine had swallowed a dose of dusty Roman summer heat along with the Three Tenors.

However, will this acoustic magic, which characterises a sports car at least as much as its autobody shape and its accelerating power, survive the years to come? [Fig. 10]

THE END OF THE AUTOMOBILE AND THE FUTURE OF THE SPORTS CAR

Digitalisation, electrification and connectivity are pushing the automobile towards the

Fig. 10: Monica Vitti and Michelangelo Antonioni during filming of *La Notte* in a Lancia Flaminia Zagato, 1961

biggest shift in its history. Cars will send signals to each other, they will feel different. In the long run, combustion engines will become the exception to the rule and maybe the same will happen to drivers. The industry dreams of autonomous, self-driving cars because if they could get rid of the driver behind the wheel, a market worth billions would open up. Once an algorithm takes control, passengers can spend their time Googling, ordering things online, writing emails and generating data. Time will tell what this transition from driving to being driven will mean psychologically and politically. The farewell to the steering wheel is a phenomenon in which we could see a huge shift in the whole of society away from freedom and self-determination as central values towards the values of comfort and safety. The design of the autonomous vehicle, unlike that of sports cars, is not shaped by the pathos of getting ahead but by the notion that the home, a piece of real estate, can be extended into the public sphere. At a time when the car becomes a covered sofa moved through the city as if by an invisible hand, the sports car will seem like a memory of an era in which the alert self-driven person who sought intensity in life was the social ideal. Will sports cars survive this transition? Maybe they will be the only ones to do so. Ecological problems and climate change are the consequences of mass motorisation, of endless lines of diesel-powered small and medium-sized cars. Sports cars, on the other hand, have always been luxury objects that have delegated questions regarding sensible everyday transport to subway systems and high-speed trains. As a result, they almost look like a model for a future in which the car is no longer a utility object reinforced with a plastic mouth in which we move at a snail's pace through rush hour to get to work, needlessly polluting the environment in the process – but an object of pleasure.

Should we not turn cars back into what they once were at the beginning of their history – objects not intended for everyday transportation (there were trains, trams, bicycles, horses and legs for that), but for fun? – Something enjoyable that was not used on a daily basis but was got out on special occasions? It is not the thing in itself but its excessive use that is the problem, polluting the air and making us weak. Nobody drives to the bakery in a sports car every day – but we would use one to do things on the spur of the moment, things we wouldn't do without a car, or if we had only some ugly means of transport.

Maybe the sports car of the period from the 1950s to the 1970s is not just a sad memory of a time when nobody really worried about climate change and safety and instead wallowed in a kind of hedonism that, from today's perspective, was inconceivably elegant.

Maybe the sports car is a glance towards the future of the automobile after the end of mass transport. Maybe cars can finally become what they once were before they also had to take on the job of bicycles, freight trains and trams: objects to create euphoria, artworks that are not used every day but that are there to encourage us in special moments to do things we would never do without them: we would not get into a diesel-powered Skoda or a Car2Go Smart car or a self-driving transport capsule to drive to Rome at one in the morning. We would do it in a sports car; we would bellow through the night-time tunnels or across the snowy passes of San Bernardino, see Lake Como flash past us in the half light, shoot under the fantastic spaceships of the Autogrill bridge restaurants in the early morning fog, leave the Autostrada Uno for a late breakfast in Piacenza before arriving with the windows down at Piazza d'Aracoeli in the early afternoon to park outside Bar Campidoglio with a sizzling engine and open the bonnet with some pomp and circumstance. That, at least, is what would happen if everything were to go well; though it could happen that a look under the bonnet became necessary around Como. Either way, whenever petrol heads touch the warm metal of the bonnet, they are always captivated by an inexplicable feeling of happiness that always seems slightly pathological to the uninitiated; the smell of hot asphalt, fuel leaking from somewhere, a pungent scent of pine resin, warm Bakelite and hot engine oil, the chatter and hum of the warmly pulsing machine can all push the petrol head into a veritable delirium that is otherwise only experienced by the religious in the frankincense haze of a Catholic Mass.

As mentioned above, this form of mobility has nothing to do with efficient travel from A to B. It is the mobility that Charles Baudelaire had in mind when he said this about 'true voyagers': 'These have passions formed like clouds; / As a recruit of his gun, they dream / Of spacious pleasures, transient, little understood, / Whose name no human spirit knows.'[8] Driving over the Julier Pass four times because it is such a joy in a Porsche Carrera, a Renault Alpine or a Lancia Stratos. Or picking someone up from the airport in Paris while living in Dusseldorf. The truth of the sports car lies in the promise that the drive could become a potentially life-changing adventure. It is not a means of transport, it is a romantic machine that catapults its driver into a different life. This adventure is not a question of money either: an Alfa Spider faded by Roman summers for 4,000 euros and a Maserati Ghibli SS (4.9 L) for fifty times that amount have several features in common: two seats, four wheels, an engine that we could listen to for hours, and a form that gives us the feeling that we have already set foot in a better world, one that is the destination of our journey. The sports car is the opposite of pragmatic locomotion: a life-intensifying experience and a consummate synaesthetic artwork embodying sound, feeling, form and speed. Perhaps the car of the future will not be an everyday utility object but an artwork on wheels, a stimulant and, even when parked, a constant source of encouragement and euphoria.

1 Jacob Burckhardt, The Civilization of The Renaissance in Italy (1860) trans. S.G.C. Middlemore, London 1878, p. 376; available online at: http://www.gutenberg.org/files/2074/2074-h/2074-h.htm (accessed July 2018).
2 Ibid., p. 377, footnote 856.
3 Quoted in Christophe Studeny, L'invention de la vitesse. France XVIIIe siècle au XXe siècle, Paris 1995, p. 54.
4 Ibid.
5 Filippo Tommaso Marinetti, Manifesto del Futurismo (1909), trans. as Manifesto of Futurism, in: Umbro Apollonio (ed.), Documents of 20th Century Art, New York 1973, pp. 19-24; online at: http://viola.informatik.uni-bremen.de/typo/fileadmin/media/lernen/Futurist_Manifesto.pdf (accessed July 2018).
6 Ibid.
7 Paul Näcke, Der Geisteszustand des Automobilfahrers, in: Archiv für Kriminalanthropologie und Kriminalistik 16, 1904, pp. 335–337.
8 Charles Baudelaire, 'Le Voyage' (1861), trans. Geoffrey Wagner as 'The Journey', in: Selected Poems of Charles Baudelaire, New York 1974.

911

CISITALIA 202 SC BERLINETTA

- DESIGNER BATTISTA 'PININ' FARINA (1893–1966)
- YEAR 1948, PRODUCED 1947–1952
- PRODUCTION RUN: APP. 170 VEHICLES
- 1.1 LITRE CAPACITY, 4 CYLINDERS, 70 HP, MAX SPEED 160 KM/H
- MANUFACTURER: COMPAGNIA MINDUSTRIALE SPORTIVA ITALIANA S.P.A., TURIN
- LENDER: TJEERD VAN DEN BERG, NETHERLANDS

The Cisitalia is an automobile. A device. A machine serving a distinct purpose. It is not a monument. This ought to be kept in mind, since the Cisitialia is usually reduced to its form, and hence its value as a mere design object, in a way few other automobiles are. This is quite understandable though, as this Italian *gran turismo* was presented as part of Philip Johnson's *8 Automobiles* exhibition at the Museum of Modern Art in New York in 1951, where it was the first of its kind to be presented on a par with the fine arts.[1] As such incisive events have the habit of being formative, the Cisitalia 202 has been viewed as more of a static sculpture than as a form of transport ever since.

So it is its form which lends the Cisitialia such significance within the automotive realm. This form was conceived by none other than the great Battista 'Pinin' Farina, founder of Carrozzeria Pininfarina and master stylist, who helped define automotive elegance like no-one else. This is reflected in his design of the Cisitalia, which was hardly minimalist, but appeared clear and clean nonetheless – especially by the standards of the year 1947, when the typical response to post-war austerity took the form of lashings of chrome and increasingly voluptuous bombast.

More than one hint that Farina had created the Cisitalia using a blank sheet of paper – literally and figuratively speaking – can be found on the car's body. Apart from its integrated, rather than separate – as was the standard at the time – wings, the 202 coupé appears almost as though it was some unbranded blueprint for the European post-war automobile in general. With hindsight, and in particularly drastic terms, one could therefore almost describe it as generic. Coupled with the fact that the Cisitialia brand has never enjoyed much in the way of a public profile, it becomes clear how the 202's design could eventually so utterly disconnect itself from the vehicle as such.

In addition to the decision – radical at the time – to eschew stylistic smoke & mirrors *à la* Detroit (disregarding the Buick-influenced side air-vents for a moment), it is the simplicity of the surfaces and the discreet proportions above all else which rendered the Cisitalia the precursor of automotive modernity. Farina may

Detail of the cockpit, Cisitalia 202 SC Berlinetta, 1948

Lancia Aurelia B20 Coupé GT, 1956

View of the exhibition *8 Automobiles*, Museum of Modern Art, New York, 1951

neither have invented the streamlined shape, nor the use of an aerodynamic form language, yet the equally moderate and elegant fashion in which he employed these stylistic devices – that is bona fide artistic mastery. It also happened to be effectively superseded only once 'Pinin' himself introduced the trapezium shape in 1957 (compare the Lancia Florida II's clear, sober outline).

To this day, the Cisitalia's two-part windscreen remains by far the clearest indicator of the design's age – an indicator that was not borne out of Farina's conception, but the technical realities of the immediate post-war period. This simultaneously illustrates just how far ahead of their time the 202 coupé and the aesthetic imagination behind it were.

Other indisputable classics, such as the Lancia Aurelia B20 GT and the Bentley R-type Continental, still drew on the Cisitalia's basic stylistic recipe years later, varying, yet by no means revolutionising it in the process.[2] Eventually, automotive design's fundamental break with Farina's Cisitalia only occurred with the introduction of the wedge shape, a good twenty years later.[3]

Once one understands this significance, it ought to be considered an obligation to grant the exceptional Cisitalia 202 the kind of status it truly deserves. Which is not that of a static monument, but that of a machine that is moving in various ways and that deserves better than paralysed reverence.

1 See Press release Museum of Modern Art, New York, 12 August 1951.
2 See Paolo Tumminelli, Car Design, Kempen 2004, p. 34.
3 See John Lamm, The Supercar: An Evolution of Speed, Osceola, WI, 2007, p. 56.

Front view of the Cisitalia 202 SC Berlinetta, 1948

FERRARI 166 MM BARCHETTA

- DESIGN CARROZZERIA FANTUZZI (1939–1993)
- YEAR 1953, PRODUCED 1948–1953
- PRODUCTION RUN: APP. 46 VEHICLES
- 2 LITRE CAPACITY, 12 CYLINDERS, 162 HP, MAX SPEED 210 KM/H
- MANUFACTURER: AUTO AVIO COSTRUZIONI FERRARI, MARANELLO
- LENDER: PRIVATE COLLECTION

Just as some canvasses carry several layers of paint on top of each other, the Ferrari 166 Mille Miglia, chassis number 0264M, possesses not merely one, but several forms.

The 'visible layer' alone of this Ferrari is arresting. Visually, it corresponds to the Barchetta design by Carrozzeria Touring, which means nothing less than that chassis 0264M boasts the archetypical body style of a Ferrari racing car.

Even though Ferrari has historically been mostly associated with designs by 'Pinin' Farina or Sergio Scaglietti, it is the Barchette created by Touring that are viewed as the definition of the *Ur*-Ferrari racing car.[1] In this context, it is not without a certain irony that the shape of the Barchetta ('little boat') – what with it having its wings integrated into the body – exhibits certain stylistic parallels to the seminal Cisitalia 202, designed by 'Pinin' Farina.

Of course, Carrozzeria Touring's design for the Ferrari 166 MM Barchetta must not be considered a mere Pininfarina copy, but an interpretation of a then groundbreaking form language *alla Milanese*. Comparing the two, the Barchetta's design appears somewhat less sober, betraying the occasional playful aspect, such as the curved lip, which runs from the front wings' extremities, alongside the headlights and then toward the upper edge of the grille, or the pronounced character line, with its rather conspicuous outline connecting the front and rear wheel arches. Quite obviously, the craftsmen at Touring did not consider it below them to give an intrinsically functional car a few decorative flourishes.

The maw found at the front of the 166 MM appears like a most rudimentary rough draft of the Ferrari grille still in use today. In terms of proportions, the strongly geometrical lattice design of the radiator grille, framed by a rounded off, barely ovoid shape, bears little resemblance to the later, definitive versions. Yet some hints of what was eventually to become the 'Ferrari style' are already detectable.

In general, the Ferrari 166 MM appears more compact and bulky than the classic Ferrari racing cars following in its wake. This is due to Carrozzeria Touring's penchant for a bit of visual lavishness, as well as the fact that the 166 MM was created right at the crossroads of pre- and post-war car design and manufacturing.

Detail of the front fender, Ferrari 166 MM Barchetta, 1953

Detail of the cockpit, Ferrari 166 MM Barchetta, 1953

So much for the Ferrari 166 MM Barchetta in general. In the specific case of chassis number 0264M, however, this description would be not just inadequate, but positively misleading. After all, this specimen did not receive its Touring-style body when it was built in 1953 – this was fitted in 1969, and not courtesy of Carrozzeria Touring, either, as the company had gone bankrupt in 1966. Instead, the then-owner of 0264M commissioned Carrozzeria Fantuzzi to give back to the vehicle what he assumed to have been its 'original' Touring body.

With hindsight, this proved to be a colossal error of judgment. For 0264M had actually been delivered with a body that could hardly have been any more exotic and exclusive. None other than Ferrari had originally built a Scaglietti-style Spider body onto chassis 0264M.[2] Which may initially sound rather dubious, as Ferrari hardly possessed the competence or facilities for car-body construction. But thanks to the support of neighbouring Carrozzeria Autodromo Modena, whose main business was the production of coachwork for buses, a handful of Ferrari bodies were built, one of which was attached to 0264M.

This kind of exceptional history would render a 'regular' Ferrari 166 MM Barchetta almost ordinary. As with certain paintings, the fascinating turns of history have the capacity to outshine pure aesthetics in this case too.

1 Giovanni Bianchi Anderloni, Carrozzeria Touring Superleggera, Milan 2016, p. 301.
2 Bjoern Schmidt, Register (9 May 2014), online at: http://www.barchetta.cc/english/All.Ferraris/Detail/0264M.166MM.53.htm (accessed 1 April 2018).

Front view of the Ferrari 166 MM Barchetta, 1953

PORSCHE 356

- DESIGN, BODY ENGINEERING ERWIN KOMENDA (1904–1966)
- YEAR 1952, PRODUCED 1948–1965
- PRODUCTION RUN 1952: 959 VEHICLES
- 1.5 LITRE CAPACITY, 4 CYLINDERS, 44 HP, MAX SPEED 140 KM/H
- MANUFACTURER: DR. ING. H.C. F. PORSCHE KG, STUTTGART
- LENDER: AUTOSTADT GMBH

The archetype of the German automotive form is not of German origin. Both the Volkswagen ('People's Car') Beetle – originally known as the KdF-Wagen, after the Nazi 'Kraft durch Freude' (Strength through Joy) movement – in its capacity as the first German mass-market automobile, as well as the German post-war sports car *par excellence*, the Porsche 356, can trace their cultural origins back to the territories that once belonged to the Austro-Hungarian empire and that later became part of the Third Reich.

Just as the 'basic architectures' of these two vehicles – both being rear-engined and driven through the rear wheels – had been devised by engineering masters Ferdinand Porsche (from the Bohemia region) and Béla Barényi (from Lower Austria), it was another native of Lower Austria, designer Erwin Komenda, who would give these basic designs their ultimate shapes.[1]

There are of course numerous intersections between the Volkswagen car, the Volkswagen brand, and the Porsche family and car brand, whereas Komenda's role has been somewhat obscured. And yet it was he who came up with the Beetle's likeable – in spite of its considerable historical burden – appearance. Furthermore, it was his duty to design the first production Porsche in 1948, which was to be based on the pre-war Typ 64 model. Developed by Ferdinand Anton Porsche, aka 'Ferry', the son of company founder Ferdinand Porsche, the 356 was originally intended to differ far more significantly from the most famous design by Porsche Sr, the aforementioned VW Beetle. However, once a prototype had been built, the plan to fit the engine between the axles was dismissed in favour of the proven rear-engine layout, to which the 356 henceforth remained loyal.[2]

This production Porsche 356 obviously conforms to the aesthetic established by the Volkswagen car, which is why one might, for simplicity's sake, call it a 'flat, smooth Beetle'. This was in part, though not solely, due to the many VW components installed in early 356 models in particular. The main stylistic influence though, apart from the existing Volkswagen design, was aerodynamics. It was in that domain where the insights Komenda had gathered while working with mathematician Josef Mickl during the development of the Porsche Typ 64 – also known as 'Berlin-Rom-Wagen' – manifested themselves.[3] As a result, early specimens of

1952
AUTOSTADT

Detail of the cockpit, Porsche 356, 1952

Porsche Typ 64, 1938/39. Built for the planned Berlin–Rome race. Features an aerodynamic aluminium body and an engine reworked to produce 40 horsepower; top speed: 140 km/h

KdF-Wagen, VW38 pre-production vehicle at the International Motor Show in Berlin 1939

the 356 appeared particularly smooth and purist, as they eschewed the majority of the Beetle's ornamentation, not to mention its separate wings and running boards.

By the standards of the early post-war years, the body style's coherent impression was as rare as it was innovative. From this perspective, the Porsche could well be considered a kindred spirit of the contemporary Cisitalia 202, which was based upon a similarly modern design approach, although the Porsche, due to its fundamentally different architecture and more matter-of-fact execution, may appear somewhat less impressive than Battista Farina's masterstroke. The 356's extremely narrow track width also makes it appear older and heavier by comparison, even though this quirk was rather widespread in those days, particularly among racing cars.

No other Porsche would ever exhibit as clean and unadorned a design as the early 356. Despite its voluminous appearance, the soft body – furnished with just windows, hatches and the most basic ornamentation – comes across as the ultimate minimalist take on the architecture upon which the Beetle was and the Porsche 911 is still based. In this context, the contrast with the Porsche's interior appears even more peculiar. Mainly thanks to the necessity to employ mass production components, the 356's cabin is characterised by the chrome-and-Bakelite look of the post-war era. Instruments, radio and ashtray all conform to the then burgeoning Americanised aesthetic of affluence, thereby marking a clean break with the ascetic style of the body.

The Porsche 356's interpretation of the unmistakeable Porsche-Beetle silhouette remains unsurpassed in its simplicity. This renders it the archetype of this most German body design that came courtesy of Bohemian-Austrian designers. One could therefore almost describe it as the stylistic nucleus of the German automobile.

1 Gerhard Stadler, Das industrielle Erbe Niederösterreichs, Vienna 2006, p. 344.
2 Brian Long, Porsche 356, Poundbury 2002, p. 15.
3 Wolfgang Fürweger, Die PS-Dynastie: Ferdinand Porsche und seine Nachkommen, Berlin 2015, p. 128.

Detail of the luggage compartment hood, front: Porsche 356, 1952

MERCEDES-BENZ 300 SL COUPÉ

- DESIGNER FRIEDRICH GEIGER (1907–1996), KARL WILFERT (1907–1976)
- YEAR 1955, PRODUCED 1954–1957
- PRODUCTION RUN SILVER: 526
- 3 LITRE CAPACITY, 6 CYLINDERS, 215 HP, MAX SPEED 225 KM/H
- MANUFACTURER: DAIMLER-BENZ AG, STUTTGART
- LENDER: PRIVATE COLLECTION

- DESIGNER FRIEDRICH GEIGER (1907–1996), KARL WILFERT (1907–1976)
- YEAR 1957, PRODUCED 1954–1957
- PRODUCTION RUN BORDEAUXROT: 15
- 3 LITRE CAPACITY, 6 CYLINDERS, 215 HP, MAX SPEED 225 KM/H
- MANUFACTURER: DAIMLER-BENZ AG, STUTTGART
- LENDER: DAIMLER AG, MERCEDES-BENZ CLASSIC [ILL. P. 17]

Legends are inevitably shrouded in a mystic veil. Automotive legends are by no means the result of magic or mere intuition, however. Instead, they are borne out of creative processes requiring the shedding of blood, sweat and tears, not to mention instinct and intelligence. The Mercedes-Benz 300 SL is no exception in this respect, even though it was and still is an exception among automobiles.

Once more, it was Austrian-American car importer extraordinaire Max Hoffman whose instinct was proven right in this case, too. For it was he who urged the decision makers in Stuttgart Sindelfingen to develop a high-performance sports car for the lucrative US market. This made sense, as this kind of vehicle would not have yielded any significant sales in Europe, which was both considerably poorer and still grappling with the aftermath of the war.

Eventually, Daimler-Benz management gave in to Hoffman's appeals and set about developing a production vehicle based on the successful 300 SL W194 racing car. Under the guidance of exceptional engineer Rudolf Uhlenhaut, a sports car, based on a tubular frame that was as light as it was rigid, was thus created.[1] This architecture did not just lend the car part of its model name – the SL standing for 'super light' – but also required a creative solution for the doors, as the sills' spatial requirements meant a conventional arrangement was not practical.[2] This resulted in the legendary gullwing doors, which are being emulated to this day. The fact that these were a functional solution in the 300 SL's case, whereas the epigones had them installed solely for the purpose of conspicuousness, is rather telling. This spirit of Swabian rationality is in evidence all over the Mercedes 300 SL – despite the need to cater to the yearning for splendour so prevalent in post-war times.

The latter fact becomes particularly clear when comparing the 300 SL to the W194 racing car, whose design is considerably simpler than the production car's and possesses a post-war chubbiness that strongly resembles that of the early Porsche 356. However, although the production 300 SL's appearance may be considerably more flamboyant, its form language avoids any sense of excess. As with almost all prestigious cars of that period, the 300 SL could hardly have eluded the influence of Americanised ornamentation. As a consequence, there

MERCEDES BENZ

Detail of the cockpit, Mercedes-Benz 300 SL Coupé, 1955

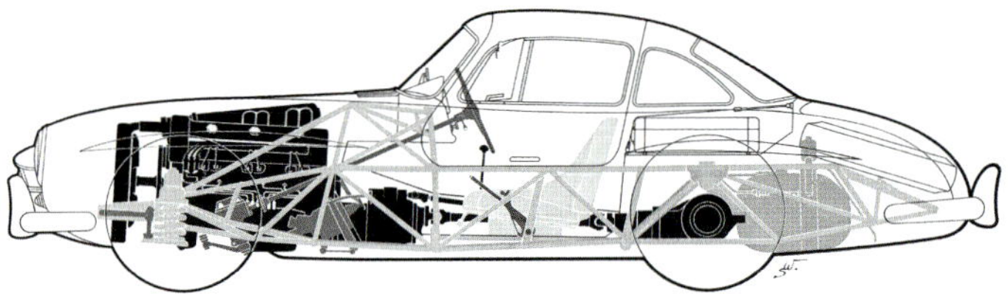

Section drawing, Mercedes-Benz 300 SL Coupé

Detail of the air vents, Mercedes-Benz 300 SL Coupé, 1955

are substantial amounts of chrome to be found all over its body, albeit not applied in such a way that they might appear vulgar.

As designed under Karl Wilbert and Friedrich Geiger, the Gullwing evades any possible accusations of kitsch thanks to the consistent application of its ornamentation: the chrome strip on the side skirts visually connects the chrome bumpers with one another, while two thin, delicately gleaming strips of chrome on the side vents subtly emphasise the horizontal line – as do the dynamic lancets above the wheel arches. The window frames, on the other hand, were simply an example of the particularly high-quality execution of a technical necessity. Similarly, the bulge on the bonnet was an effect of another engineering requirement, as the height of the right-hand side inlet manifold necessitated the additional bulge on the left in order to create a symmetric appearance.

Equally high-quality, yet practical, was the cabin, which was fitted with a tilt-away steering wheel and plaid-cloth seats as standard, even though most customers would not be deterred by the surcharge and chose the optional leather seats regardless. Similarly 'Benz-like' in the proverbial sense was the colossally solid, high-quality fittings.

As it turned out, it was the 300 SL's front end that ultimately proved to be the more influential feature designed by Wilfert's stylists than the gullwing doors. For more than six decades, evolutionary takes on this grille design – a soft trapezium shape, tapering towards the bottom – adorned the front ends of the vast majority of Mercedes sports cars and coupés, before it recently had to give way to a far more aggressive interpretation of the theme. Even legends are not sacrosanct, after all.

1 See Wolfgang Scheller, Thomas Pollak, Rudolf Uhlenhaut. Ingenieur und Gentleman, Königswinter 2015, p. 16.
2 Online at: https://www.zeit.de/mobilitaet/2017-04/mercedes-konzernarchiv-autogeschichte-dokumentation (accessed 7 May 2018).
3 See Anthony Pritchard, Gullwing, London 2008, p. 56.

Front view with open gullwing doors, Mercedes-Benz 300 SL Coupé, 1955

LANCIA AURELIA B24 S AMERICA SPIDER

- DESIGNER BATTISTA 'PININ' FARINA (1893–1966)
- YEAR 1955, PRODUCED 1954–1955
- PRODUCTION RUN: 240 VEHICLES
- 2.5 LITRE CAPACITY, 6 CYLINDERS, 118 HP, MAX SPEED 185 KM/H
- MANUFACTURER: LANCIA & C., TURIN
- LENDER: PRIVATE COLLECTION

Whenever one moves within the sphere of what is generally acknowledged as beautiful, details and nuances gain the utmost significance.

During the 1950s and 1960s, the business model of Carrozzeria Pininfarina could simply and comprehensively have been described as 'beauty'. Company founder and chief designer, Battista 'Pinin' Farina, understood how to employ the visual perfect pitch with which he was gifted in order to produce enchanting automotive forms on a regular basis. This proverbial 'good taste', which could easily be viewed as an altruistic service to the automobile world, thus became the trademark of the Turinese company.

As many automobile manufacturers wanted to benefit from this good taste, 'Pinin' Farina's style continued to spread – particularly among Italian high-end marques, one of which was Lancia, back in the day.

Just like most other European manufacturers of distinction, this formidable luxury brand from Turin was intent on succeeding in the profitable US market during the post-war period. For this reason, Lancia and Pininfarina – aided by influential importer of European cars, Max Hoffman – conceived of a Roadster (*scusi:* Spider!), aimed at establishing the spirit of *la dolce vita* in the New World. The matter of this Spider's appearance was handed to Pininfarina for the aforementioned reasons.

The result was of course beautiful, as was to be expected. Very beautiful even, in a way that suggests it is more of an outright Pinin Farina than a Lancia creation. Yet, for all its virtuosity, it was not just the Farina line that made this Lancia Aurelia B24 Spider something special, but the corresponding details and nuances.[1]

The tiny doors without handles; the steering wheel that corresponds with the angle of the wraparound windscreen's frame; the chrome line alongside the sills that visually connects the bumpers and is interrupted only by the haunches above the rear wheel arch – these are the subtleties that distinguish the Lancia from other descendants of the Farina stable's Cisitalia 202 bloodline. Not to mention the unashamedly American panoramic windscreen, which has such an utterly different effect when surrounded by sleek Turinese elegance rather than by chrome-plated American rocket-age baroque.

Detail of the cockpit, Lancia Aurelia B24 S Spider America, 1955

Lancia obviously formed a union that was simply meant to be. At least during that special moment towards the end of the 1950s.

Since then, the Aurelia B24 Spider's values have skyrocketed. Today, it is considered a bona fide gem of an automobile, quite in contrast to the lamentable fate of the Lancia brand. The Lancia Aurelia Spider's exceptional significance can be found in the many small details, the nuances, and the cohesiveness with which it all adds up to something exceptional – thanks to a special alliance of Turinese excellence.

1 Michael Frostick, Pininfarina – Architect of Cars, Deerfield, IL, 1978, p. 64.
2 Paul Schinhofen, Lancia – Innovation und Faszination, Königswinter 2006, p. 89.

Leaving any stylistic details aside, it ought to be stated that, in terms of shared ideals, Pininfarina and Lancia were a closer match than some of the better-known collaborations of the *carrozzeria*. For what united these two noble enterprises – certainly when they were at the peak of their respective capabilities – was a casual, discreet striving for excellence, which manifested itself not just in the Lancia Aurelia Spider, but especially in the seminal Lancia Florida and Lancia Florida II concept cars, which were created during the same period.[2] Battista 'Pinin' Farina, the man, as well as Pininfarina, the company, and

Front view of the Lancia Aurelia B24 S Spider America, 1955

ALFA ROMEO GIULIETTA SPIDER

- DESIGNER BATTISTA 'PININ' FARINA (1893–1966)
- YEAR 1956, PRODUCED 1955–1964
- PRODUCTION RUN 1956: 2,141, TOTAL APP. 14,300 VEHICLES
- 1.3 LITRE CAPACITY, 4 CYLINDERS, 55 HP, MAX SPEED 160 KM/H
- MANUFACTURER: ALFA ROMEO S.P.A., PORTELLO
- LENDER: PRIVATE COLLECTION

The Alfa Romeo Giulietta Spider possesses countless qualities. Most prominent among them is the fact that this Alfa contributed to the process of automotive democratisation – and the manner in which it did so. At the same time, it also helped establish the Italian coachbuilders, the *carrozzieri*, in the global market.

Of course, the Giulietta Spider was never a truly inexpensive vehicle – its exquisite engineering alone saw to that. And yet it enabled quite a large group of buyers to achieve what had hitherto seemed impossible: to drive an Alfa Romeo – and an open-top one at that – as a 'commoner'. After all, just a few years before, the Milanese marque had been exclusively purveyors of the most sophisticated means of motoring to the aristocracy. Just as the designs by Carrozzeria Pininfarina had embodied the privilege of the privileged.

With the Giulietta Spider's unveiling, the joys of an Italian automobile of the highest order may not have become readily available to the masses, but certainly to far more people than the usual motorist elites. Stylistically, this simultaneously marked the breakthrough for the Pininfarina style, from the realm of exclusive coachbuilding into mass manufacturing. Incidentally, the Giulietta Spider was also the first mass-market car built by Pininfarina.

Albeit no 'pocket-sized Ferrari' by any means, the Giulietta Spider's unadorned flanks clearly betray the relation. Foregoing the kind of embellishments and bulges that were standard at the time, and instead relying utterly on its expertly modelled surfaces, this Alfa stands for the Italian style as largely created by Pininfarina, which was on the cusp of conquering the world. Romantic, but by no means baroque; reserved, but not clinical. This form language, coupled with the engineering finesse Alfa Romeo provided, enchanted the US market to such an extent that American importer Max Hoffman declared he could sell as many Giulietta Spiders as Pininfarina was capable of building.[1] A burgeoning appreciation of Italian car design ensued, which would result, a decade later, in the Americans – hitherto undisputed, often copied global champions in the field – bringing vehicles to market that had clearly been inspired by the Turinese style.

This quiet yet impactful kind of success was very much in keeping with the Giulietta Spider's character. After all, it was hardly the

Detail of the Cockpit, Alfa Romeo Giulietta Spider, 1956

Sophia Loren in an Alfa Romeo Giulietta, around 1958

most spectacular representative of Pininfarina's form language,[2] what with its relatively compact proportions featuring a rather short bonnet and an almost centrally located cabin. However, it proved to be among the most popular, which also illustrates the adaptability of the style created by Battista Farina, which simply worked – regardless of price and body shape.

Style was not the only Italian export merchandise Pininfarina's Spider helped break through. It was the concept of the Italian mid-size, open-top sports car in general that would be successfully adapted – not solely, but primarily – by Alfa Romeo for decades to come. For this reason, the 'Spider' monicker bears a clear Italian connotation, even today (in spite of its British origin, where it traditionally described particularly light sports carriages without substantial body).

There may have been more spectacular, more elegant and altogether more visually significant Italian vehicles from this period. And yet the Alfa Giulietta Spider plays a special role among the body of work of Carrozzeria Pininfarina and Battista Farina, insofar as its characteristic shell shape became the source of inspiration for various other sports cars. In that sense, this Alfa turned out to be not just an attainable object of desire for an entire generation, but also a propitious ambassador for the Italian way of life, Milanese engineering and Turinese design skills.

1 See Maurizio Tabucchi, Alfa Romeo From 1910 to 2010, Vimodrone 2010, p. 45.
2 See Michael Frostick, Pininfarina – Architect of Cars, Deerfield, IL, 1978, p. 67.

Front view of the Alfa Romeo Giulietta Spider, 1956

BMW 507 FACTORY PROTOTYPE

- DESIGNER COUNT ALBRECHT VON GOERTZ (1914–2006)
- YEAR 1955, PRODUCED 1956–1959
- PRODUCTION RUN SERIES MODEL: 254
- 3.5 LITRE CAPACITY (SERIES 3.2), 8 CYLINDERS, 185 HP (SERIES 150 HP), MAX SPEED 220 KM/H
- MANUFACTURER: BAYERISCHE MOTORENWERKE AG, MUNICH
- LENDER: PRIVATE COLLECTION

The story of the BMW 507 is told rather quickly. Intended to be the Bavarian response to the groundbreaking Mercedes-Benz 300 SL, the 507 roadster was supposed to instantly establish the still war-affected Bayerische Motorenwerke as purveyors of glamorous luxury motor cars – particularly in the affluent North American market.

In actual fact, the 507's lack of sales success eventually contributed to an intensification of the crisis threatening BMW's existence.[1] Even in terms of prestige, the Gullwing Mercedes remained safely beyond the Bavarians' reach – that is until BMW themselves paid homage to the 507 with the most exuberant gesture of reverence imaginable, in the shape of the Z8 retro roadster. This finally enabled the progenitor car to join the Pantheon of classic cars, forty years after production of the 507 had ended.[2]

The history of the 507 factory prototype bearing chassis number 70.003 is not told quite so quickly. In the beginning, the projected BMW roadster was supposed to get a completely different design from the one eventually put into production. The equally soft and bulky appearance of this first prototype bore more resemblance to a pre-war racing car than a luxury sports car for the post-war period of economic boom. Max Hoffman, influential importer of BMWs into the US, was accordingly alarmed and made it abundantly clear that he would not be able sell such a car. In the same breath, he recommended German-American product designer Count Albrecht von Goertz. The nobleman had not designed a car by that point, but instead had had a previous engagement at the then highly prestigious studios of Raymond Loewy.[3]

The Bavarians and the count quickly struck a deal, after which von Goertz presented a proposal that was drastically different from the clumsy first version. Von Goertz had combined the sleek silhouette of the Le Mans racing cars of the time with the kind of opulent detailing that was *de rigueur* in those days. However, even the count's design is not without its idiosyncrasies. The immense wheels in particular, which are barely housed by the BMW's body and protrude from the wheel arches in peculiar fashion, appear somewhat curious, whereas the plump rear wings, which include more than a hint of tail

Detail of the cockpit, BMW 507, 1955

BMW Roadster 507, series model, 1956

fins, suggest some American influence on von Goertz' creation.

Prototype No. 70.003 indeed suggests that this effect was fully intentional on the stylist's part. For 70.003 differs from the later production cars in certain details, such as front wings, which are longer and pointier towards the headlights. At the same time, the bumpers are more delicately executed than the production 507's, thus adding further emphasis to the wheels' visual heft. The lack of a chrome handle on the boot lid, as well as the taller fins, also allows certain conclusions to be drawn as to the way in which von Goertz' original design was subsequently adapted by his clients. In the case of the production car's significantly less complex front grille, this is very clear indeed: it was obviously changed to avoid unnecessary complexity.

It is open to question, to say the least, that it was the changes implemented after 70.003 had been built that prevented the BMW 507 from attaining greater sales success, simply because these changes are too subtle to have made a marked difference. And yet 70.003 grants an interesting insight into the aesthetics of Count Albrecht von Goertz – not to mention the car's fascinating history.

Years after the 507's development had ended, touring car champion and BMW test driver Hubert Hahne happened across the mothballed prototype in the BMW factory's catacombs. This led him to express a desire for the car – a request BMW eventually granted in November 1970. Since then, 70.003 has changed hands only twice. Next to the 254 examples of the production 507 roadster, 70.003's status as von Goertz' *Ur*-design obviously renders it a particularly special specimen of the breed.

1 See Horst Mönnich, The BMW Story: A Company in Its Time, London 1991, p. 410.
2 See Tony Lewin, The BMW Century: The Ultimate Performance Machines, Minneapolis 2016, p. 155.
3 See Axel Wülfing, Der BMW 507 Werksprototyp 70.003, Schwelm, p. 10 (private edition AW).

Front view of the BMW 507, 1955

ALFA ROMEO GIULIETTA SPRINT SPECIALE (SS) PROTOTIPO

- DESIGNER FRANCO SCAGLIONE (1916–1993)
- YEAR 1957, PRODUCED 1959–1966
- PRODUCTION RUN SERIES MODEL: 1.366
- 1.3 LITRE CAPACITY, 4 CYLINDERS, 100 HP, MAX SPEED 190 KM/H
- MANUFACTURER: ALFA ROMEO S.P.A., PORTELLO
- LENDER: COLLEZIONE LOPRESTO

Giorgetto Giugiaro and Marcello Gandini were by no means the first masters of design to emerge from Carrozzeria Bertone. Before these two *Wunderkinder* revolutionised automotive design in the late 1960s and '70s, a barely less talented stylist by the name of Franco Scaglione was in charge of the forms coming from the coachbuilder in Grugliaso near Turin.[1]

The prime example of Scaglione's body of work from that period is the Alfa Romeo Giulietta SS Prototipo. In contrast to the later production car based on it, this iteration even does without the traditional Scudetto, the Milanese marque's shield-shaped grille, which usually houses the Alfa Romeo emblem. However, the form language Scaglione had established at Bertone is clearly in evidence. Like some kind of biomorphic, rocket-powered UFO, the Giulietta SS Propotipo appears as though it does not depend on its wheels at all. Were it not for the appendages above its front wheels and the (by the standards of its time) restrained use of chrome, this red body could almost be taken for some kind of softly organic, sanded phenomenon. As a matter of fact, this particular form language happened to be Scaglione's speciality – some four decades before it would become known as 'soft design' and dominate the automotive industry for several years, thanks to modern mass manufacturing techniques. In sharp contrast to this, the vehicles based upon Scaglione's drafts were laboriously handmade, as there was no other way to cast such vast, soft forms in aluminium.

It must be said, though, that the Alfa Romeo is not entirely unorthodox, but abides by certain classical stylistic instruments, such as the haunches above the rear wheels. Yet, when combined with the short wheelbase, the dramatically bowing roof – which also provokes with its 'incorrectly' placed apex far ahead of the driver's head – and the low headlights, which are placed like cones at the tips of the rocket-shaped wings, an overall impression far beyond classical ideals of beauty prevails.

In more than one way, the Giulietta SS Prototipo also acted as a link between Scaglione's outré B.A.T. (Berlinetta Aerodynamica Tecnica) concept cars and the production Giulietta Sprint Speciale, as it followed

Giulietta
speciale

Detail of the interior, Alfa Romeo Giulietta Sprint Speciale (SS), 1957

in the Prototipo's wake. With each step towards roadworthiness, the expressive extravagance was successively watered down and adapted to more popular aesthetic ideals. The Giulietta SS Prototipo therefore appears borderline conventional next to one of the B.A.T. Alfas, whereas it comes across as rather daring when compared with the Giulietta Sprint Speciale production version.[2]

Despite its strong character, the Giulietta SS Prototipo's form itself was influenced by role models, just as it was to become a source of inspiration to others itself. Like everybody else within the car design world back in those days, Franco Scaglione would have turned west for inspiration when spotting the newest trends. For during the 1950s, the centre of the automotive design realm was located in Detroit, Michigan. And it was there, particularly at General Motors, where the kind of automotive shape that would ideally have shaken off the archaic concept of the wheel in order to concentrate on nuclear-powered, rocket-shaped, chrome-heavy means of transport was created. This spirit, interpreted in typically Italian *sprezzatura* fashion, is also in evidence on the Giulietta SS Prototipo, albeit in a lighter, simpler form, with Scaglione's billowing surfaces added on top.

This composition, which appears so coherent in its entirety, would eventually become a source of inspiration for the stylists of Coventry, England, where Italian designers' talents were generally highly regarded. It is therefore hardly a coincidence that some of the Giulia SS Prototipo's cues would be found – sometimes in adopted, sometimes in newly interpreted fashion – on the legendary Jaguar models that were unveiled the following decade.[3] Giorgetto Giugiaro, then a very young designer – and soon to be a very big name in the industry – similarly did not erase all the traces of his predecessor Scaglione during his first years at Bertone. Talent borrows, genius steals.

1 See Giuliano Silli, Franco Scaglione Designer, Turin 2010, p. 15.
2 See Andrew Nahum, Fifty Cars that Changed the World, Design Museum London, London 2009, p. 46.
3 See Nick Hull, Jaguar Design – A Story of Style, Worcestershire 2015, p. 163.

Front view of the Alfa Romeo Giulietta Sprint Speciale (SS), 1957

FERRARI 250 GT CALIFORNIA SPYDER

- DESIGNER SERGIO SCAGLIETTI (1920–2011), BATTISTA 'PININ' FARINA (1893–1966)
- YEAR 1960, PRODUCED 1957–1962
- PRODUCTION RUN: APP. 104 VEHICLES
- 3 LITRE CAPACITY, 12 CYLINDERS, 240 HP, MAX SPEED 240 KM/H
- MANUFACTURER: AUTO AVIO COSTRUZIONI FERRARI, MARANELLO
- LENDER: PRIVATE COLLECTION

In 2008, Ferrari introduced an all-new, rather clumsily styled folding metal roofed convertible. It was named California.[1] Fifty-one years prior to this, the name had been lent to another Ferrari: the 250 GT California Spyder. Within the ramified 250 model range, this variant was tasked with conjuring up a bit of glamour, which led to the Spyder being named not just after one of its main markets, but also as an homage to the west coast state's symbolic significance as the cradle of modern, avant-garde chic at the time.

In that spirit, this Ferrari would carry the jet set from their John Lautner homes in Hollywood to their Richard Neutra-designed Palm Springs retreats in classical European style. Which appears only appropriate, given the fact that the American automobile was still in the late stages of its futuristic chrome baroque era, whereas the Californian elite had already discovered a more restrained aesthetic.

Taking all of this into account, the clean, elegant lines of the Pininfarina-designed, Carrozzeria Scaglietti-built Ferrari, appear entirely consistent.[2] For the Turinese masters of design had come up with yet another variant of the Farina line, which possessed instant appeal – particularly in the case of the short-wheelbase version, which was introduced in 1960. With its discreet haunches, the unobtrusive side air vent, the slim rear and glass-covered headlights, the California bore all the typical hallmarks of a Pininfarina effort, without any significantly deviation from the style of other contemporary designs by the *carrozzeria*. This extends to the cabin as well, where a delightful row of gorgeous gauges yet again upholds the banner of sleek, simple elegance – and does its utmost to distract from the rather rudimentary design of the door cards. All things considered, the California's cabin meets one's expectations and therefore delights – without much in the way of surprises, however.

The characteristics that allow the Ferrari 250 GT to excel therefore ought to be found in areas other than sheer aesthetics. For example in the field of motor sports, where its successes garnered the California Spyder a status exceeding that of the pretty boulevard cruiser. Or in the combination of the athletic yet dignified Farina line with the unique driving appeal of the Tipo 125 V12 engine that was installed

Detail of the cockpit, Ferrari 250 GT California Spyder, 1960

Alain Delon and Jane Fonda in a Ferrari 250 GT California Spyder

in all 250 models. All in all, the combined appeal of these attributes created the basis for the California myth's crucial component: the glamour of the bold and the beautiful.

Stars such as Paul Newman, Steve McQueen, James Coburn and James Garner were spotted behind the California Spyder's wheel - all of them household Hollywood names who happened to be talented racing drivers as well. In this instance, the motto was not so much 'to see and be seen' as 'to be seen and adulated'.

Provided with badges of approval, courtesy of Scuderia Ferrari (the company's racing team), Pininfarina, the racing world in general and Hollywood, the 250 GT California Spyder was inevitably destined to mature into an automotive legend. And yet the splendour this kind of nimbus entails can also turn into a burden. For example when selling prices put the automobile itself into their shadow. Or when the California monicker is exploited decades later to sell a barely related product of dubious aesthetic quality to unsuspecting customers.

The latter arrangement actually does the younger California quite a disservice, too: after all, there is no shame in not living up to a legend – however, giving it a try in the first place is, at the very least, folly.

1 See Robert Foskett, Ferrari 308, 328 and 348, Marlborough 2015, p. 127.
2 See Michael Frostick, Pininfarina – Architect of Cars, Deerfield, IL, 1978, p. 71.

Front view of the Ferrari 250 GT California Spyder, 1960

MASERATI 5000 GT ALLEMANO

- DESIGNER GIOVANNI MICHELOTTI (1921–1980)
- YEAR 1963, PRODUCED 1959–1964
- PRODUCTION RUN: 34 VEHICLES
- 4.9 LITRE CAPACITY, 8 CYLINDERS, 340 HP, MAX SPEED 270 KM/H
- MANUFACTURER: SOCIETÀ ANONIMA OFFICINE ALFIERI MASERATI, MODENA
- LENDER: PRIVATE COLLECTION

Exclusivity is relative. What is considered beautiful, good and precious today would have been considered an above-average commodity half a century ago. At best.

In sharp contrast, a total production figure of thirty-four units was always considered truly exclusive. This is the total number of Maserati 5000 GTs built, which must then be divided by the different body styles it came in, courtesy of the finest stylists Italy had to offer at the time. No matter if one is talking of Pietro Frua, Pininfarina, Giorgetto Giugiaro at Bertone or Sergio Sartorelli at Ghia: they all, and quite a few others on top, had a go at designing a form to put on top of the 5000 GT's chassis.

Given these circumstances, one cannot help but come to the conclusion that the Maserati 5000 GT has nothing whatsoever in common with today's luxury automobiles of the global moneyed elites. Instead, it was a vehicle fit for a prince, a king or any other kind of excellency who was able to appreciate not just what was expensive, but what was exceptional. Which ultimately manifested itself in the figure of no more than thirty-four automobiles, wearing decidedly varying costumes. At least in terms of quantity, the most successful among these body designs was the one envisaged by industrious stylist Giovanni Michelotti. His creation, christened 'Indianapolis', was built no less than twenty times by Carrozzeria Allemano, with each specimen featuring discreet variations.[1]

Michelotti's thus only moderately exclusive design suited to a T the aristocratic Modenese marque with the *tridente*, which traditionally made the Italian competition appear almost plebeian in terms of status and reputation in those days. The flair of this obscenely expensive, sensationally fast *gran turismo* is accordingly genteel – quite in contrast to the first and most famous 5000 GT by the way, the oddly opulent, Touring-designed *Scià di Persia*.[2] Thanks to its almost saloon-like silhouette, the Allemano Maserati maintains a certain degree of stateliness, which, at least in part, counteracts the Maserati's ludicrous road performance – *noblesse oblige*. Yet at the same time, its proportions obviously leave no doubt as to the potency of this Modenese machine, for no regular car could ever wear so small a passenger cabin and so much of a bonnet at once. This impression of measured decadence

Maserati 5000 Bertone, 1961

Maserati 5000 GT Ghia, 1961

Detail of the cockpit, Maserati 5000 GT Allemano, 1963

continues when studying the stylistic details. In keeping with the far more common BMWs and Triumphs Michelotti penned over the years, the designer remained true to the ethos of disciplined elegance. Thus prominently placed decorative panels are conspicuous by their absence. The chrome that is present is used in incisive fashion instead, in order to highlight certain elements, such as the light units, air vents and windows. Apart from this, brightwork is only to be found in the same spots as on any run-of-the-mill car of the time: on handles, levers or emblems. However, the style of an aristocrat such as the Maserati must obviously not enter the realm of the banal. For that reason, it not only adorns itself with the aforementioned exceptional proportions, but also with the decorative insignia of exclusivity. This is particularly evident on its canopy, which is supported by wafer-thin pillars and visually dominated by the extensive wraparound rear window. This roof, together with the discreet, horizontal tail fins, are the only cases of blatant ornamentation Michelotti granted his 5000 GT. After all, a status symbol completely devoid of splendour would be rather oxymoronic. Yet from today's perspective, this Maserati for crowned heads is indeed hard to grasp. Its exclusivity did not serve an ulterior purpose, but was an end in itself. The Maserati brand thus gained glory, but neither additional income nor the kind of image gain that could be monetarised. *L'art pour l'art.*

1 See Maurizio Tabucchi, Maserati, Königswinter 2004, p. 223.
2 See Martin Buckley, Maserati, Sparkford 2011, p. 81.

Front view of the Maserati 5000 GT Allemano, 1963

FERRARI 250 GT SWB BERLINETTA COMPETIZIONE

- DESIGNER BATTISTA 'PININ' FARINA (1893–1966), SERGIO SCAGLIETTI (1920–2011)
- YEAR 1961, PRODUCED 1959–1962
- PRODUCTION RUN 1961: 73 VEHICLES
- 3 LITRE CAPACITY, 12 CYLINDERS, 240 HP, MAX SPEED 260 KM/H
- MANUFACTURER: AUTO AVIO COSTRUZIONI FERRARI, MARANELLO
- LENDER: PRIVATE COLLECTION

If there was a single combination of numbers at the very core of the oft-quoted *mito* Ferrari (Ferrari legend), it would be *duecentocinquanta* – two-fifty. For it was the 250 models that turned Ferrari into the epitome of the ethereal sports car and Modena into the Mecca of automobile enthusiasts the world over. Much of this was naturally due to the three-litre Tipo 125 V12 power unit, as designed by engineering genius Gioacchino Colombo, whose swept volume of 250 cubic centimetres per cylinder lent the model range its name.

Yet the meaning of Ferrari's 250 models is also founded upon their rich diversity, what with Ferrari being able to cover the entire spectrum of two-door automotive glamour with these vehicles. Road and track-race cars, *gran turismo* and spider models – everything Ferrari ideally stands for can be found within this range of automobiles.

In that context, the 250 SWB Berlinetta embodies three attributes in outstanding fashion: power, performance and beauty. Despite having been devised as a racing car and having proven itself successful in this area, the 250 SWB is, from today's perspective, a classical beauty first and foremost. Its body, designed by Pininfarina and built at Scaglietti, is exemplary of the aesthetic values of both Scuderia Ferrari and master stylist Battista 'Pinin' Farina.[1] Therefore, its proportions are appropriately classical, with a long bonnet, elegant haunches and restrained decorum.

No matter if the bumpers are fitted or taken off for racing: the Ferrari 250 SWB Berlinetta's stance is sublime – and not just because of its shortened wheelbase, which is reflected by the SWB acronym and does the car's silhouette an awful lot of good. Its visual presence is anything but clumsy, just as it is devoid of any unnecessary ornamentation, as worn by previous, far more baroque, 250 model variants or by its glamorous Lusso siblings. All of which results in an enchantingly sleek, almost matter-of-fact elegance, which is not based on opulence, but on measured reduction. Regardless of this, all add-on components fitted to the 250 SWB, be they headlights, door handles or light units, are standard parts that could be found not just on other Ferraris, but in some cases on humble, mass-produced vehicles, too. Yet the way in which these were integrated into the SWB

Rear view of the Ferrari 250 GT SWB, 1961

Fender detail, rear, Ferrari 250 GT SWB, 1961

Berlinetta and help facilitate the Ferrari's glorious basic shape would render any allegations of supposed cost-cutting measures a case of outright infamy.

The single fly in this ointment: the air vents behind the front wheels' put-on appearance, which was overlooked by the likes of Ferrari, Pininfarina and Scaglietti, and should grate on owners and spectators alike. In this case, a flush, sleek visual solution would theoretically have been preferable. But of course there is no excellent beauty without some strangeness to it, according to Francis Bacon.[2]

Lacking any oddity whatsoever is the 250 SWB's cabin, which may be the cleanest, most delicate and simply the prettiest to ever grace a Ferrari's inside. Seven round Veglia gauges in two sizes, a row of toggle switches, some leather and a bit of stainless steel are all it takes to create a cockpit of graphical clarity and noble minimalism. In this case, too, the stylists and artisans relied on the fundamental correctness of the design and just left it alone at the right moment. For this reason, the Ferrari is among those few motor cars whose interior and exterior shapes form an utterly coherent whole.

Coherence generally is the virtue that allows the SWB Berlinetta to excel not just among the 250 models or Ferraris in general, but any kind of sports car. Its form, which basically was yet another evolutionary take on the Farina line, became the benchmark, thanks to its consistent interpretation of the classic Ferrari-Farina style.

1 See Michael Frostick, Pininfarina – Architect of Cars, Deerfield, IL, 1978, p. 90.
2 See Richard Whately, Bacon's Essays – With Annotations, Boston/New York 1871, p. 433.

Front view of the Ferrari 250 GT SWB, 1961

ASTON MARTIN DB4 GT ZAGATO

- DESIGNER ERCOLE SPADA (B. 1938)
- YEAR 1962, PRODUCED 1960–1963
- PRODUCTION RUN: 19 VEHICLES
- 3.7 LITRE CAPACITY, 6 CYLINDERS, 314 HP, MAX SPEED 246 KM/H
- MANUFACTURER: ASTON MARTIN & ZAGATO
- LENDER: PRIVATE COLLECTION

The relationship between artist and audience is complex. What constitutes a masterpiece to one may be a banality to the other. And vice versa.

With the Aston Martin DB4 Zagato,[1] a very young, budding designer by the name of Ercole Spada created a vehicle that has been apotheosised by automotive aficionados ever since its unveiling in 1960. To Spada himself, the *créateure*, the Aston constituted but an insignificant early work, which he had designed right after having been hired as Carrozzeria Zagato's chief designer. This assessment appears surprising only at first glance, however. A closer look reveals that this DB4 lacks not just the *codatronca* (Kamm) tail that really was essential for Spada's body of work then, but also his penchant for the discreetly whimsical.

The Aston Martin DB4 Zagato is a typical Italian sports-car design, in the best sense of the term – as well as a restrained representative of the Zagato breed. Which does not come as a surprise, considering the Milanese *carrozzeria* had not been tasked with making the Aston prettier, but more competitive on the race track.

With this in mind, the designer changed everything about the body that was not strictly necessary – apart from the 'broad hips' of its rear aspect, which Spada considers an oversight to this day. The *doppia gobba* canopy so typical of Zagato racing cars was conspicuous by its absence, though – only the three bulges on the bonnet come across like some kind of homage to that trademark feature.

The old-fashioned tail fin stubs, on the other hand, were deleted without replacement, as they were a bit of an anachronism by the early 1960s. The entire body of the DB4 became more compact and organic in order to save weight. For the same reason, it also received Perspex windows and aluminium cladding. The latter was not just the work of Spada, but the result of Milanese artisanship above all else. For the Zagato tinsmiths truly understood how to treat alloy bodies like nobody else: before grinding the body panels, these were painted black, that way achieving an equally thin and smooth finish, which contributed to the DB4 Zagato's exceptionally soft appearance.[2]

Spada's Aston does without both bumpers and chrome decorum. The small amounts of

Rear side view of the Aston Martin DB4 GT Zagato, 1962

Fiat Abarth 750 Zagato, Doppia Gobba, 1955/56

brightwork on it are merely discreetly glistening, thin slivers of metal around the light units, windows and air vents. By the standards of the time, this constitutes a case of bona fide aesthetic minimalism.

Yet the Aston Martin DB4 Zagato's appearance is by no means ascetic. Thanks to its relatively compact body, the Zagato seems pleasingly proportioned, certainly not haggard, but almost cuddly. This impression is due to the rather luscious forms just as much as the slightly droopy frontal aspect, which features generous glazing over the headlights. Not to mention the pert rear and its four tiny light units. All these features combined result in a lack of visual aggression that marks a charming contrast to the rather masculine image of this automotive legend. Which leads straight back to the definitive answer to the initial question: Whose assessment of the Aston Martin DB4 Zagato is the correct one – the artist's or the audience's? Are we dealing with a banality or a masterpiece?

As is so often the case, coming up with a definite statement is rather pointless. What is certain is that the attractiveness of this Zagato is of a different kind from that of Spada's latter-day designs; maybe a bit easier on the eye and less idiosyncratically technocratic. But that does not render it banal.

This is also the reason why the Aston Martin Zagato is so particularly coveted. It is less challenging than other, more consistent, Zagato creations. Yet at the same time, the proverbial and actual Italian *leggerezza* certainly suits this rather stiff Brit well. And that's that.

1 See Ulrich Bez, Making Aston Martin, Kempen 2013, p. 60.
2 See Bart Lenaerts and Lies de Mol, Spada, Bielefeld 2014, p. 32.

Front side view of the Aston Martin DB4 GT Zagato, 1962

JAGUAR E-TYPE COUPÉ PRESENTATION VEHICLE GENEVA MOTOR SHOW 1961

- DESIGNER WILLIAM LYONS (1901–1985), MALCOM SAYER (1916–1970)
- YEAR 1961, PRODUCED 1961–1974
- PRODUCTION RUN: 7,670 VEHICLES
- 3.8 LITRE CAPACITY, 6 CYLINDERS, 265 HP, MAX SPEED 240 KM/H
- MANUFACTURER: JAGUAR CARS LTD., COVENTRY
- LENDER: DR. CHRISTIAN J. JENNY, THALWIL, SWITZERLAND

His research and development department's newest creation did not exactly stir up an awful lot of enthusiasm in Sir William Lyons. Acting not just as the founder and managing director, but also as chief designer of Jaguar, Lyons considered sports cars a distraction from the main business of building and selling saloon cars. He accordingly kept his elation well in check when his chief engineer, Bill Heynes, and aerodynamicist, Malcolm Sayer, showed him a new roadster model.

With that car, Sayer had obviously refined his design of the D-type racing car[1] into a shape that was less compressed, with less protruding haunches on the wings and an even longer bonnet, featuring a 'power dome' – a bulge at its centre, to accommodate the tall XK six-cylinder engine. What remained the same, though, was the almost prudish track width. All things considered, Sayer, whose automotive shapes were based on mathematical formulae, had created an obscenely stylised roadster. The almost caricature-like bonnet, the flat rear, and the despite their scientific origins – unquestionably sensual curves would mark the stylistic high point of this kind of motor car. To this day. But for Sir William, Jaguar's boss, the E-type became relevant only once a coupé needed to be developed, using the roadster as basis.[2] Together with his assistant, master tinsmith Bob Blake, Lyons set to work – without the help of mathematics, instead relying upon his visual judgement and unerring good taste. The result of this typically Lyonesque *modus operandi* was a far more strongly curved canopy than usual, complete with the carried-over steep windshield, as well as the sensational 'coffin' rear hatch. The latter's side hinges were the result not of a stylistic epiphany, though, but of sheer necessity, as the E-type's roof was simply not solid enough to facilitate a hatch that hinges upwards. The combination of Sayer's streamlined racing aesthetics and Lyons' sense of tasteful flamboyance resulted in the Fixed Head Coupé (as it was officially called) becoming the *primus inter pares* among early E-type models. Also because Sir William stayed true to himself in every way: despite being a penny-pincher of the highest order, the Jaguar founder was more than willing to pay for even the smallest of details as long as there was some aesthetic merit to them. This can be observed on

Rear view of the Jaguar E-type, 1961

Detail of the cockpit, Jaguar E-type, 1961

the E-type FHC's rear end, where no unseemly creases or shutlines interrupt the flow of the wing into the canopy and back. Trifling matters like the lack of a seam- or shutline entail a lot of expensive manual labour, but distributed significant visual dividends.

Much to Sir William's astonishment, the E-type not only became the star of the Geneva Motor Show in 1961, it turned into a veritable phenomenon. The 'penis on wheels' suited the Swinging Sixties like no other sports car, and not due just to any sexual connotations in its proportions. On top of that, the E-type was significantly cheaper than any competition that could hope to keep up with it in terms of performance and style, which rendered it at least ever so slightly egalitarian. In terms of complementing the hedonism, as well as the emerging pop cultural domination of Great Britain, the E-type was without equal anyway – so it hardly came as a surprise when the Jaguar was originally destined to become the company car of James Bond. But as the enormous demand for the E-type had resulted in production shortages, Sir William rebuffed the production company's request, which resulted in the Aston Martin DB5 getting the gig as 007's motor in *Goldfinger*. The more the E-type was stylised as a phenomenon of the *zeitgeist*, the less it appeared to lend itself to any adaptations. Two revisions and a regrettable 2+2 variant, featuring more commodious interior accommodation, as well as a disfigured silhouette, attested to just how much the design quality and impact of this supposedly ostentatious piece of styling ultimately

Jaguar D-type "short nose", Malcolm Sayer and Norman Dewis, 1955

Jaguar E-type, presentation vehicle, Geneva Motor Show, 1961,
2nd from the right Jaguar co-founder Sir William Lyons,
3rd from the right Rudolf Uhlenhaut, engineer at Mercedes-Benz

depended upon delicate details. It was this quality that persisted, as the E-type phenomenon faded away, along with the swing of the sixties, and became a regular automobile. And that is still true today.

1 See Stephen Bayley, Cars. Freedom, Style, Sex, Power, Motion, Colour, Everything, London 2008, p. 210.
2 See Nick Hull, Jaguar Design – A Story of Style, Worcestershire 2015, p. 158.

Front side view of the Jaguar E-type, 1961

FACEL VEGA II

- DESIGNER JEAN DANINOS (1906–2001)
- YEAR 1962, PRODUCED 1961–1964
- PRODUCTION RUN: 184 VEHICLES
- 5.9 LITRE CAPACITY, 8 CYLINDERS, 390 HP, MAX SPEED 214–225 KM/H
- MANUFACTURER: FORGES ET ATELIERS DE CONSTRUCTION D'EURE-ET-LOIR, S.A., PARIS
- LENDER: PRIVATE COLLECTION

Despite *égalité* being part of the national creed, French society is hardly at odds with the good life, much to the benefit of the domestic gastronomy sector, not to mention the tourism and luxury foodstuffs industries. However, when it comes to the automobile, a preference for equality suddenly manifests itself. For whoever wants to drive about in luxurious fashion needs to shop at the import car brands.

Of course, over the course of French automotive history, a number of illustrious makers of sports and luxury cars did emerge, such as Bugatti, Talbot Lago, and Facel. The latter constituted a serious attempt at establishing an exceptional French luxury marque.

As with other daring enterprises, Facel was the creation of a single determined individual – in this case by the name of Jean Daninos. Acting as the company's founder, managing director, chief engineer and designer all at once, he created Facel (Forges et Ateliers de Construction d'Eure-et-Loir) automobiles, which were extensively hand-built and based on his own taste.[1] Far removed from the avant-garde lightness of touch of a *grande* Citroën or the exquisite opulence of a Bugatti, Daninos' Facel Vega models exuded an incomparable interpretation of automotive luxury. Based upon the conservative basic architecture of the three-box coupé, his Facel Vega II captivated through its flamboyant details, such as the elongated rear lights sitting on top of barely insinuated tail fins. This kind of balancing act also manifests itself through the use of stainless steel, which is employed in huge quantities, yet in a stylistically restrained fashion. The rather voluminous appearance of the Vega II's wings and doors create a stark contrast to the lithe canopy, which is supported by only the most delicate of stainless-steel pillars. Even the aforementioned tail fins are executed with the kind of formal elegance of a contemporary Pierre Cardin suit and subsequently appear hardly brash or vulgar. The interior is defined by contrasts as well. Levers, gauges and buttons are spread across a dashboard whose fine wood-grain is a literal example of *trompe-l'œil* – an illusion, hand-painted onto bare metal, and hence proof of craftsmanship of the highest order.[2]

The Facell II's particular elegance is mostly due to its lowered roof, which lends the car a

Detail of the cockpit, Facel Vega II, 1962

cowering, racy silhouette. This is coupled with a driving performance that shamed a great many far sleeker contemporary sports cars. This inimitable combination of luxury, taste, aesthetics and athleticism turned the Facel II into one of the finest cars not just of its time.

The downfall of the manufacturer Facel SA in 1964 was caused not just by the smaller Facellia model, which failed in the marketplace and whose unreliability destroyed the marque's reputation, but also the much publicised accidental death of novelist and philosopher Albert Camus, who perished on the passenger side of a Facel Vega HK500, piloted by publishing heir Michel Gallimard, in 1960. That one of France's great intellectuals would die in the country's most luxurious motor car, of all places, was too tragic to bear. The end of Facel hence also marked the end of Jean Daninos' very own luxury automobile concept.

Such in many respects singular sports cars would be as unimaginable in today's luxury sector as a France that is more concerned with automotive than with Lucullan pleasures. After all, there still are some absolute terms that can be relied upon.

1 See Obituaries: Jean Daninos, in: The Daily Telegraph, London, 3 November 2001.
2 See Jean-Paul Chambrette, Dominique Bel, Michel Renou and Michel Revoy, Facel Vega: Der große französische Grand Tourisme, Königswinter 2016, p. 312.

Front view of the Facel Vega II, 1962

AC SHELBY COBRA 289

- DESIGNER ALAN TURNER, AC CARS LTD.
- YEAR 1964, PRODUCED 1962–1965
- PRODUCTION RUN: 655, RIGHT-HAND DRIVE: 45 VEHICLES
- 4.7 LITRE CAPACITY, 8 CYLINDERS, 400 HP, MAX SPEED 260 KM/H
- MANUFACTURER: AUTO-CARRIERS LTD, THAMES DITTON
- LENDER: PRIVATE COLLECTION

The Shelby Cobra's status among the world's finest sports cars is special indeed. Rather than being a noble thoroughbred, the Anglo-American automotive beef-cake is more of an ordinary mongrel. But just as in the animal kingdom, this crossbred is, in fact, in many ways more robust and capable than quite a few exquisite studs. Instead of an elegantly complex V12 engine, all the Cobra needed for setting drag-race records and winning races was the sledgehammer-like might of a rather simple Ford V8 unit. Instead of automotive *couture à la* Pininfarina, Ghia or Touring, this sports car made do with the chubby, slightly uncouth roadster shape of the British AC Ace it is based upon, which had been the creation of Alan Turner. It was thanks to the business acumen of American former racing driver Carroll Shelby that in 1962 the AC Ace, a rather crude British sports car, became the Cobra, a bona fide automotive legend.[1] Prior to that, Shelby had registered the potential in the AC's simple, light and robust ladder-type chassis frame. For this enabled the British roadster to withstand the enormous power of the Ford engine Shelby intended to install.

The might of this power unit manifested itself accordingly in the Cobra's appearance. Wide and rowdy, with enormous extended wheel arches, as necessitated by the massive tyres, which are in turn a necessity if the V8 engine's potency is to be mostly turned into traction. Next to the contemporary European competition, but also when compared to the conceptually more similar Corvette, the Cobra appears rather stout.

That the Cobra's copiousness does not veer towards the bombastically vulgar is due to the car's surfaces being devoid of decorum: no seam, no swage has been placed for the sake of it. The air vents, lids and bumpers similarly betray a sense of expedience. At the same time, the Cobra is free from any kind of ornamentation, such as unnecessary spoilers or sill extensions – or, in a figurative sense, it lacks tattoos and shave-off hair decoration. The Cobra could therefore be compared to a boxer of the traditional ilk: squat, powerful, but not exactly elegant.

As a matter of fact, it is this blue-collar flair that lends the Shelby Cobra its appeal. Particularly as this can be interpreted as the antithesis to the aristocratically arrogant

Detail of the rear with towing device, AC Shelby Cobra 289, 1964

Detail of the cockpit, AC Shelby Cobra 289, 1964

attitude of the European sports-car elite in those days. Rather than failing to imitate the establishment using simple means, the Cobra was all about achieving the objective of bringing as much power as possible onto the road and race track in the most economical way possible. And exactly this kind of sober sincerity is reflected through the design – regardless of those plump curves.

A side effect of this simplicity, however, is that the Cobra's body shape can be all too easily replicated. This in turn means that only a fraction of the Shelby Cobras one encounters on the road, all over the globe, are the real thing;[2] most examples truly are just replicas or other, less significant variants. However, even these circumstances could not prevent the Cobra legend from growing, and even resulted in a particular kind of connoisseurship which prides itself for being able to identify a 'real' Cobra.

As simple as the wide, loud, fast Shelby Cobra may be, the myth it established is as manifold and unique. And that is the measure by which the value of a sports car is ultimately gauged.

1 See Carroll Shelby and John Bentley, The Cobra Story, New York 1965, p. 18.
2 See Colin Comer, Shelby Cobra Fifty Years, Minneapolis 2011, p. 230.

Front view of the AC Shelby Cobra 289, 1964

PORSCHE 911

- DESIGNER FERDINAND ALEXANDER PORSCHE (1935–2012)
- YEAR 1967, PRODUCED 1964–1973 (ORIGINAL MODEL)
- PRODUCTION RUN 1967: 1,599 VEHICLES
- 2 LITRE CAPACITY, 6 CYLINDERS, 130 HP, MAX SPEED 210 KM/H
- MANUFACTURER: DR. ING. H.C. F. PORSCHE KG, STUTTGART
- LENDER: PETER BRÄUER

Identifying the Porsche 911 itself amid the '911 myth' is nigh on impossible. Too manifold are the legends surrounding Germany's favourite sports car, too inflationary the hymns of praise. In order to approach the 911 as a vehicle and design object therefore requires a bit of effort – and an extremely level-headed point of view.

The *Elfer*'s unique silhouette, as designed by Ferdinand Alexander Porsche in 1963, is one of the true icons of automotive design – to this day, and with good reason. Once again, the most German concept of dogged evolutionary improvements has proven its worth, as the Porsche is clearly an epigone of Erwin Komenda's design of the VW Typ 1, *the* prototype of German mobility.[1] On the one hand.

On the other hand, the *Elfer*'s shape itself was adapted over the course of five decades, albeit with a clear focus on preserving certain characteristics. Thus the 911 and its form language became part of the national heritage to some, and plain sacrosanct to others. Which explains the kind of furore caused when Porsche dared to experiment with the shape of the round headlights in the late 1990s. Such dense fog, consisting of tradition, pop culture and myth making, only clears when observed from the aforementioned level-headed point of view. And from there, far more prosaic reasons for the *Elfer*'s long-lasting success come to the fore. Such as its rear engine, which also had such a profound effect on its body's shape.

Taking the orthodox perspective, the rear-engined design was a matter of keeping the brazen Porsche tradition intact, which had been established with the VW Typ 1 and was then continued with the Porsche 356 after the war. This view is correct, at least in part. Yet at the same time, one ought to take into account the fact that this rear engine also brought about the practical benefit of a relatively large cabin. And it was this feature that lent the 911 above-average everyday usability, certainly by sports-car standards.[2] More than all those myths and legends, it is this advantage of the Porsche's architecture that prevented the *Elfer* from ever going out of fashion or becoming obsolete. Ultimately, it helped it to become the factotum of the sports-car realm. Of course, it is this architecture that also defines the Porsche 911's visual appearance. Its combination of low, wide tail and rather short front constitutes the biggest

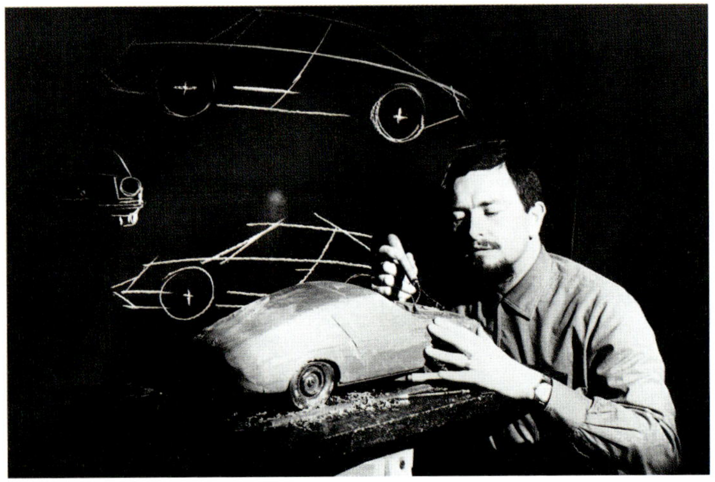

Ferdinand Alexander Porsche with a Porsche 911, no year

Detail of the cockpit, Porsche 911, 1967

tangible difference between the *Elfer* and the rest of the sports-car fold. And that is despite the fact that its rather long overhangs should theoretically foil any impression of athleticism. However, even upon its unveiling, the audience's eyes had already been adjusted to this kind of appearance – thanks to the VW 'Beetle' and its derivatives.

In general, the Porsche 911 constituted a clearly evolutionary piece of design, even when it was first introduced. Thanks to larger windows and a wider, more contemporary track width, the *Elfer* appeared far less portly than its immediate predecessor, the Porsche 356, but kept that car's soft, mostly smooth surfacing intact. All light units, air vents and the likes kept their original position and were only modernised in terms of proportion and form. These relatively straightforward changes to Komenda's *Ur*-design proved to be sufficient[3] to shed the 356's sedate, slightly baroque aura and to lend the 911 a clarity that was fully in keeping with the upcoming *zeitgeist*. Similarities to Dieter Rams' formative Braun product designs, which were about to set standards, are obvious. [Fig. p. 28] Yet the 911, particularly with regards to its still staid interior, did not adhere to the Ulmer Schule's ideals of functionality with the same kind of consistency as Rams' works.

Without continuous development, the *Elfer* would never have attained the status of *primus inter pares* among sports-car legends. For only its longevity has made it truly immortal.

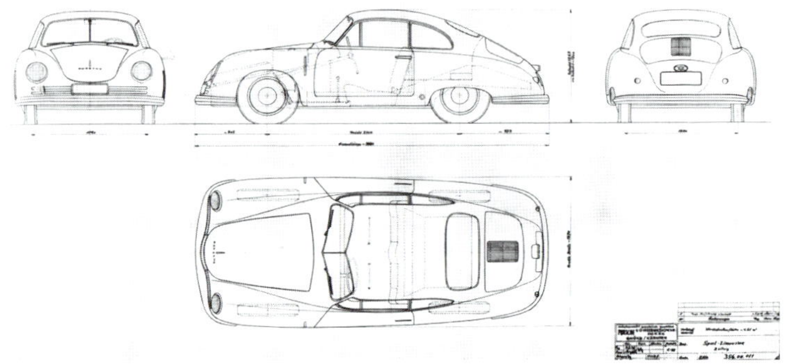

Design drawing, Porsche 356/2 Coupé, 1949

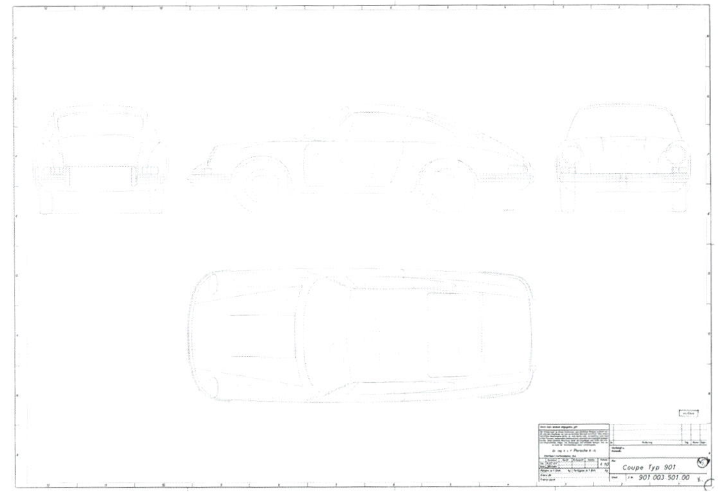

Design drawing, Porsche 901/911 Coupé, 1962

1 See Markus Caspers, Designing Motion. Automotive Designers 1890 to 1990, Basel 2016, p. 124.
2 Sam Livingstone, The Porsche 911 Was Not Designed Around Its Rear Engine (16 June 2015), online at: https://petrolicious.com/articles/the-porsche-911-was-not-designed-around-its-rear-engine (accessed 20 March 2018).
3 See Karl E. Ludvigsen, Porsche – Origin of the Species, Cambridge 2012, p. 38.

Front view of the Porsche 911, 1967

BIZZARRINI GT STRADA 5300

- DESIGNER GIOTTO BIZZARRINI (B. 1926)
- YEAR 1968, PRODUCED 1964–1968
- PRODUCTION RUN: APP. 120 VEHICLES
- 5.4 LITRE CAPACITY, 8 CYLINDERS, 370 HP, MAX SPEED 280 KM/H
- MANUFACTURER: AUTOMOBILI BIZZARRINI S.P.A., LIVORNO
- LENDER: SCUDERIA TREDICI MONACI

The engineer and designer Giotto Bizzarrini is one of the legendary names in Italian sports-car engineering. After having worked at Alfa Romeo, Ferrari and Lamborghini during the 1950s, he established his own design and manufacturing company (Automobili Bizzarrini SpA) in Livorno in 1962. At first his business focused on outside contracts in the areas of vehicle design and engine development. In addition to working with Ferrari, he also had a close working relationship with the car manufacturer Iso, owned by the Rivolta family from Milan. Among many other models, he constructed the four-seater Iso Grifo on behalf of Iso Rivolta, on which he based a racing version that was initially produced and sold by Iso as the Grifo A3/C (for Competizione) from 1963 onwards. Yet in 1965, the business relationship with Renzo Rivolta came to an end, though Bizzarrini was able to continue production of this racing car in his own name – now called Bizzarrini GT 5300. In order to expand his entrepreneurial activities, he came up with the idea of developing a road-legal version of the racing vehicle: the Bizzarrini GT Strada 5300 sports car.

In actual fact, Bizzarrini's design can barely be described as a 'sports car's'.[1] For what it truly constitutes is a racing car for the road. That much is already clear when taking even a quick glance at its extreme proportions, which make strikingly few concessions to ergonomics and practicality. The Bizzarrini's idiosyncratic physiognomy is provocative: neither its short bonnet – despite it being front-engined – nor its extremely long, flat roof adhere to conventional ideals of sports-car beauty, which usually feature elongated bonnets and elegantly tapering rears. In sharp contrast, the Bizzarrini's roofline does not form a harmonious unity with the boot lid at all. In light of this, it is hard to give credence to the speculation that the GT Strada 5300's form was significantly influenced by Carrozzeria Bertone and its lead designer at the time, Giorgetto Giugiaro.[2] What appears more likely is that the Bizzarrini's raw, machine-like form, which features so few aesthetic traits, was the brainchild of Bizzarrini and his assistant Piero Vanni, and that Bertone at best contributed modest refinements to its styling.

Of course, the Bizzarrini does sport curved fenders, air intakes and outlets, as well as

Detail of the front fender, Bizzarrini GT Strada 5300, 1968

Alfa Romeo Stradale 33, 1967

round, glazed headlights. Or, in short: several of the markers of 1960s sports-car design. Yet in the GT Strada 5300's case, their use seems to be motivated by the manufacturing techniques of the time, rather than by aesthetic requirements. Hence the headlights' covers appear to be at slightly too steep an angle to truly flow in the wind. Or the windows' placement, which comes across as somewhat random. Not to mention the fact that, apart from the fenders, there are no lines on the Bizzarrini's body that flow without some kind of interruption.

However, criticising Giotto Bizzarrini's design for its visual shortcomings would be short-sighted indeed. For it is precisely this slightly awkward nature that lends the GT Strada 5300 its unique appeal. It may seem much less smooth and ornate a design than the aesthetically related Alfa Romeo 33 Stradale. But it is exactly this hardly slick and ever so slightly rough-and-ready appearance that renders the Bizzarrini such an unusual specimen in the category of so-called road racing sports cars.

1 See Winston Goodfellow, Bizzarrini: A Technician Devoted to Motor-Racing, Vimodrone 2004, p. 36.
2 See David Trauer Adolphus, Pebble Beach 2013: 1965 Bizzarrini 5300 GT Strada Alloy (19/08/2013), online at: https://www.roadandtrack.com/new-cars/news/a5220/go-news-pebble-beach-2013-1965-bizzarrini-5300-gt-strada-alloy/ (accessed 22 March 2018).

Front view of the Bizzarrini GT Strada 5300, 1968

FERRARI 275 GTB/4

- DESIGNER BATTISTA 'PININ' FARINA (1893–1966), SERGIO SCAGLIETTI (1920–2011)
- YEAR 1967, PRODUCED 1964–1968
- PRODUCTION RUN: 330 VEHICLES
- 3.3 LITRE CAPACITY 12 CYLINDERS, 320 HP, MAX SPEED 280 KM/H
- MANUFACTURER: AUTO AVIO COSTRUZIONI FERRARI, MARANELLO
- LENDER: PRIVATE COLLECTION

A legend must not reflect reality. After all, its essence is exaggeration. And being blindly adulated. A legend therefore ought to dazzle, flaunt and sometimes even confuse.

In the automotive domain, there is no greater legend than that of Ferrari, the marque and its products. Among the best examples on whose basis this can be proven and explained is the Ferrari 275 GTB/4. Its design is, even by Ferrari standards, considered to be exceptional, significant and, above all, pretty. Among the great Ferrari models, the 275 GTB/4 ranks near the top. It accordingly arouses an almost boundless longing.

Indeed, its provenance could hardly be any more noble, as the legendary *carrozzieri* Pininfarina and Scaglietti were both involved in the design process of the 275 models.[1] Their supposedly simply task had been to clothe a typical Ferrari chassis in attractive attire, which, in the case of this hand-built sports car, rear-wheel-driven and powered by a Colombo V12-engine, would not necessarily appear too daunting a task. However, once the legend surrounding it has been subtracted from the Ferrari 275 GTB/4, its aesthetics are hardly beyond the shadow of a doubt. Of course the oval grille, long bonnet, slanted gills and sloping tail are not only clear cyphers for the generally aspirational category of sports car, but undoubtedly also correspond to the ideals of a classic Ferrari, as established by the preceding 250 model range in particular.[2] However, the 275 GTB/4 possesses a notable plumpness that would appear to be at odds with the image of athletic European elegance. Its silhouette similarly comes across as rather stocky, its wings – due to the astoundingly small wheels – as a bit podgy. The luscious hips in turn cause a visual domino effect, which renders the rear lights smaller than the Ferrari norm, just as with the front grille, though in that case exacerbated by the oversized headlight glazing. In conjunction with the small windows and the steeply raked windscreen, the roof, which is not tapering particularly elegantly towards the trailing edge, creates a somewhat compressed silhouette, which would typically suggest American provenance, rather than *lo stile italiano.*

All things considered, the 275 GTB/4's Pininfarina body appears rather progressive – and almost uncouth. And that probably is the

Detail of the air vents, Ferrari 275 GTB/4, 1967

attraction to many. The delicacy and almost feminine aura of certain other Ferraris of the era – particularly those in whose design Aldo Brovarone had some say – is utterly conspicuous by its absence here. This Ferrari is ever so slightly on the rough side, some of its details appear even a bit simple, and not just by Pininfarina's standards. Yet to some, this lack of elegance and grace is no bane, but boon. Maybe this is also among the reasons for the market rating the 275 GTB/4 rather higher than numerous other, equally rare, but far 'prettier' designs from Turin and Maranello.

However, ascribing the Ferrari 275 GTB/4's allure entirely to its virile flair would be misleading. For its true beauty is in how it embodies the power of the Ferrari legend like no other product of this proud house. After all, beauty lies in the eye of the beholder only in the case of regular automobiles. Such rules do not apply to legends.

1 See Markus Caspers, Designing Motion. Automobildesigner von 1890 bis 1990, Basel 2016
2 See Antoine Prunet, Pininfarina: Art and Industry, 1930–2000, New York 2000, p. 198.

Front view of the Ferrari 275 GTB/4, 1967

LAMBORGHINI MIURA P400
LAMBORGHINI MIURA S SERIE II

- LAMBORGHINI MIURA P400
- DESIGNER MARCELLO GANDINI (B. 1938)
- YEAR 1968, PRODUCED 1966–1973
- PRODUCTION RUN: 475 VEHICLES
- 3.9 LITRE CAPACITY, 12 CYLINDERS, 350 HP, MAX SPEED 280 KM/H
- MANUFACTURER: AUTOMOBILI FERRUCCIO LAMBORGHINI, SANT'AGATA BOLOGNESE
- LENDER: SCUDERIA TREDICI MONACI

- LAMBORGHINI MIURA S SERIE II
- DESIGNER MARCELLO GANDINI (B. 1938)
- YEAR 1970, PRODUCED 1966–1973
- PRODUCTION RUN: 140 VEHICLES
- 3.9 LITRE CAPACITY, 12 CYLINDERS, 370 HP, MAX SPEED 280 KM/H
- MANUFACTURER: AUTOMOBILI FERRUCCIO LAMBORGHINI, SANT'AGATA BOLOGNESE
- LENDER: PRIVATE COLLECTION

Who designed the Lamborghini Miura? Few questions excite the world of classic-car design to the same degree as this one. Which hardly comes as a surprise, considering not just one of the great classic cars of all time is involved, but also the two most famous designers the automotive realm has ever known: Marcello Gandini and Giorgetto Giugiaro.

What is beyond all question is that the Miura heralded one of the greatest changes in car design history on its unveiling in 1966. On top of that, it defined the category of supercar and consequently became an instant icon. Almost as though encapsulating the spirit behind the establishment of the Lamborghini marque, the Miura did not merely challenge the competition, it positively show it up.[1] No Ferrari and no other Lamborghini could match its extravagance. Not in terms of engineering, but particularly not when it came to styling.

The Lamborghini chassis' rear mid-engine layout may have been influenced by motor racing, but its shape was solely dedicated to the spectacular, rather than to lap times or aerodynamics. While a lot more masculine in its appearance than most other sports cars of the 1960s, the Miura proved to be hardly averse to the odd bit of make-up. No matter if the slats at the rear, the doors and around the headlights or the hexagonal lattice behind the engine bay are concerned: in the Miura's case, function is usually required to follow form. In the case of this superlative object, the capacity as a means of transportation was considered secondary. Of far greater concern was the ability of the forms to move.

And that they truly did. Thanks to its flat, muscular body, whose rolling hips and extended pillars appear sinewy rather than sensuous, the Lamborghini possessed the proportions of a hardened athlete. But due to the lavishly applied make-up, it exceeded the status of sports car and evolved into a supercar. The engine bay's spectacular hatch, and opened doors that resemble the outline of a bull's horns, would appear almost superfluous in that regard. But the Miura features these too, of course.

Whoever actually designed the Lamborghini Miura down to its smallest detail is an appropriately exciting question, given the importance of this piece of design. For

Side view of the Lamborghini Miura P400, 1968

Side view of the Lamborghini Miura S Serie II, 1970

Side view with opened bonnet and front, Lamborghini Miura P400, 1968

Detail of cockpit, Lamborghini Miura S Serie II, 1970

Detail of motor block, Lamborghini Miura S Serie II, 1970

decades, the genius behind the Miura's forms was thought to be Marcello Gandini, who had devised an instant classic with his first job in the capacity of Bertone chief designer – being not even thirty years old by that point. That Gandini ended up churning out masterpiece after masterpiece over the ensuing decade supported that impression, even though the Miura resembles Gandini's later style more in terms of the execution of the ornamentation rather than in the body's basic modelling.

Decades later in an interview,[2] Giorgetto Giugiaro, Gandini's predecessor at Bertone and design legend of equal stature, referenced the existence of the design for a Bizzarrini race car that his successor supposedly used as a template for the Miura. Thus, the competition between these two titans reached another level. Giugiaro had scale models built on the basis of those Bizzarrini/Miura blueprints he had left at Bertone, to which Gandini replied by devoting an entire chapter in his biography to the subject, in which he went about refuting Giugiaro's claims in nauseating detail.[3]

To onlookers, this argument might well appear either amusing or undignified. Yet the very fact that two of the greatest automotive stylists of all time vehemently claim authorship of a particular design showcases the significance and quality the flamboyant, spectacular, drastic, unique Lamborghini Miura's form possesses.

In case Giugiaro had truly been responsible for the basic shape, whereas Gandini delivered the decorum, one would not only need to thank the two of them for this sensational design – but the stroke of luck that brought their talents together.

1 See Joe Sackey, The Lamborghini Miura Bible, Poundbury 2008, p. 24.
2 Guy Bird, Designer Interviews: Giorgetto Giugiaro (3 Dec. 2012), online at: http://cardesignnews.com/media/imported/199676/199676.html (accessed 29 Apr 2018).
3 See Gautam Sen, Marcello Gandini – Maestro of Design, vol. 2, Deerfield, IL, 2017, p. 173.

Detail of engine with bonnet raised, Lamborghini Miura P400, 1968

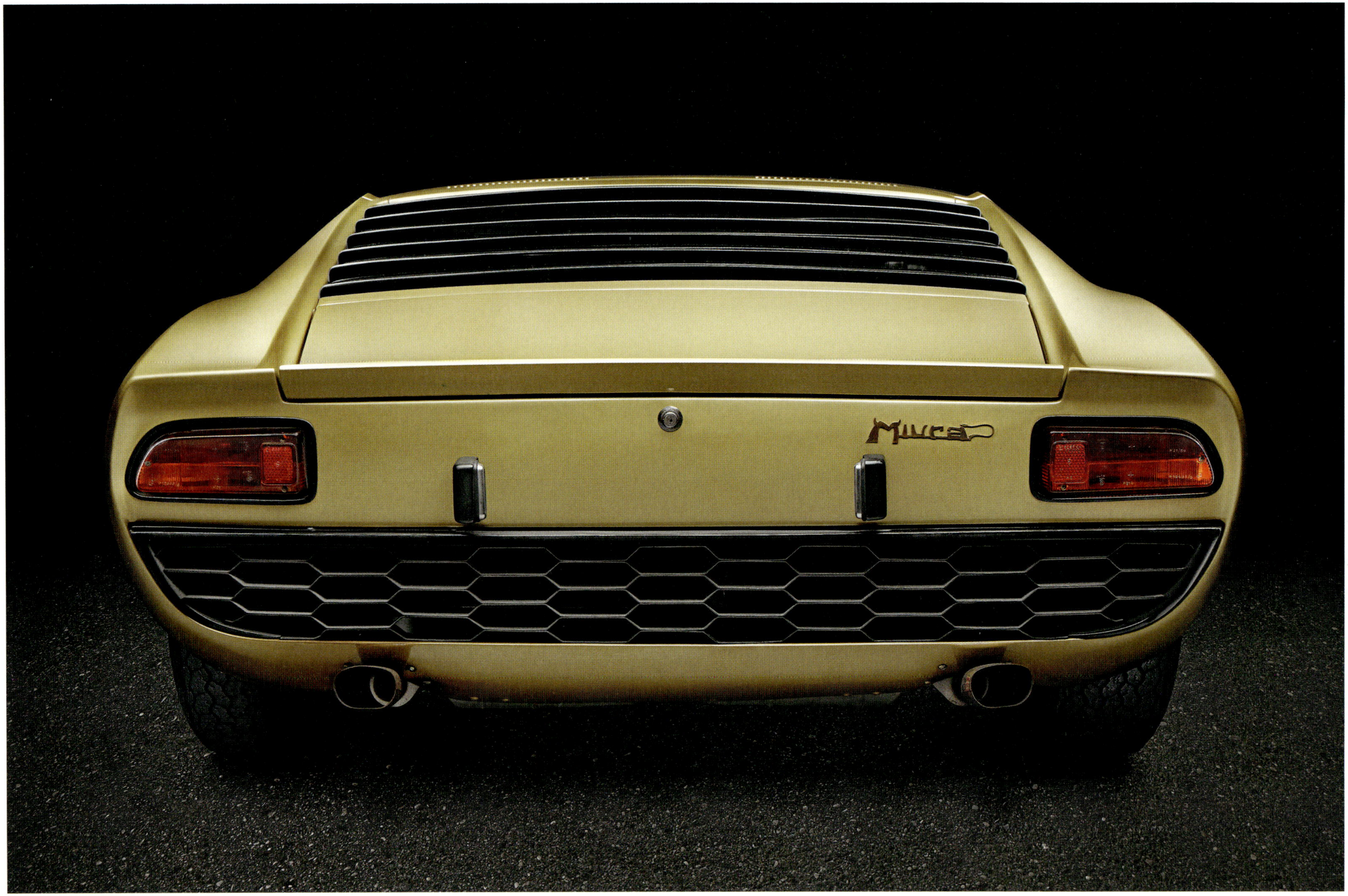

Rear view of the Lamborghini Miura P400, 1968

Front view of the Lamborghini Miura S Serie II, 1970

DE TOMASO MANGUSTA

- DESIGNER GIORGETTO GIUGIARO (B. 1938)
- YEAR 1967, PRODUCED 1967–1971
- PRODUCTION RUN: 400 VEHICLES
- 4.7 LITRE CAPACITY, 8 CYLINDERS, 305 HP, MAX SPEED 245 KM/H
- MANUFACTURER: DE TOMASO MODENA S.P.A.
- LENDER: RESTAURATION FERDINAND P. GMBH, WILLICH

Alejandro de Tomaso was a man of many talents: ambitious racing driver, ruthlessly shrewd businessman, scoundrel. The one constant throughout his enterprising career was a consistent refusal of doctrines. Everything de Tomaso touched was compromised. The one thing that mattered to him was that, at the end of the day, he had some kind of result – in the shape of a deal or marketable product – to show.

Even though de Tomaso was neither engineer nor stylist, his attitude eventually left traces on the numerous vehicles he was responsible for. This, in a way, became a stylistic trademark. A trademark that could also be found on the De Tomaso Mangusta. Thought up as a quick (in many ways) response to the Shelby Cobra and the Ford GT40, the Mangusta was supposed to combine race-car performance with Italian flair and the robustness of an American power unit – at a comparatively moderate price. In order to lend this intention an aesthetic shape, de Tomaso hired the services of Carrozzeria Ghia,[1] whose chief designer in those days was none other than Giorgetto Giugiaro.

Giugiaro used the basic chassis De Tomaso provided, whose design was not too dissimilar from the Lamborghini Miura's or Ford GT40's, to create a shape that was less technoid than the American car's and less exuberant than that of the competition from Emilia Romagna. The gullwing hatches Giugiaro devised for the rear engine bay obviously constituted an unashamed *divertissement*, but next to the Lamboghini's ornamentalism, the De Tomaso – what with its three discreet gills behind the side window – appears almost sober. In fact, the tidiness of the Mangusta's sufficiently tense surfaces, the few, but precisely placed lines, seams and creases are most reminiscent of the Maserati Ghibli that Giugiaro had also designed while at Ghia. In direct comparison, the De Tomaso may lack a bit of refinement, but that does not distract from its overall impressive stance.

However, the clean form language Giugiaro employed during his Ghia years required attention to detail in order to be at its most effective. Unfortunately, attention to detail is a quality the Mangusta sorely lacked. The – even by Italian standards – idiosyncratic panel gaps and the occasionally clumsy

Maserati Ghibli, Tipo AM 115, 1967–1973

Ford GT40, 1963–1968

use of chrome make it abundantly clear that the De Tomaso is no style icon of the traditional Italian ilk. Its charms are more reminiscent of an Adriano Celentano than a Marcello Mastroianni. The latently rough aura the Mangusta exudes was, one could be led to assume, less rooted in Giugiaro's talents than in the way in which his design was translated into production. At the same time, though, it is this same lack of perfection that lent all De Tomaso products their particular appeal.

Among the patriarch's regular and impulsive decrees, emulation of the competition, adoption of trends in record time, or the niching of markets ranked at the top of the list. The results of this approach ultimately never ended up flawless and were, in some cases, even utter folly – and yet they all symbolically stood for Alejandro de Tomaso's unpredictable, irrepressible drive. In the Mangusta's case, this meant that De Tomaso had banked on the revolutionary mid-engined chassis design a full six years before Ferrari would do so. Not in a thorough and considerate manner, but impulsively and hurriedly, the underdog having thus recognised the future of the sports car for what it was and acted.

This approach was hardly compatible with that of the Mangusta's designer, though. The different stances towards quality might have played a role in Giugiaro's decision to leave his post at Ghia, right after the *carrozzeria* had been taken over by none other than Alejandro de Tomaso.[2] Which makes the Mangusta also a memento of a brief, fruitful collaboration of two enormously different, highly creative minds.

1 See Giuliano Molineri, Giorgetto Giugiaro. The Genius of Design, Milan 2015, p. 84.
2 See Daniele Pozzi, De Tomaso: From Buenos Aires to Modena. The History of an Automotive Visionary, Deerfield, IL, 2016, p. 71.

Front view of the De Tomaso Mangusta, 1967

TOYOTA 2000 GT

- DESIGNER SATORU NOZAKI
- YEAR 1967, PRODUCED 1967–1970
- PRODUCTION RUN: 351 VEHICLES
- 2 LITRE CAPACITY, 6 CYLINDERS, 150 HP, MAX SPEED 193 KM/H
- MANUFACTURER: TOYOTA MOTOR CORPORATION, TOYOTA
- LENDER: TOYOTA DEUTSCHLAND GMBH

Japan is not merely striving and fastidious.[1] Japan is also proud. This pride is the reason why the Toyota 2000 GT exists.

By the dawn of the 1960s, Japan was by no means a global power. But the foundation for future success had been laid. Which was good enough a reason for the domestic industry to think about something other than everyday business for the first time: prestige. Ideally in the form of proof of its abilities, in a rarefied manner.

In the case of Toyota, the industry leader, this opportunity arose rather spontaneously. Out of the blue, the company was approached by Yamaha, the Japanese conglomerate with an interest in the automotive field, in order to present a project for the creation of a sports car that had already been envisaged as a partnership with Nissan, a project which ultimately fell through. At Toyota, whose success came at the price of an image that made the brand synonymous with dull mass-market fare, such an offer was obviously welcomed with open arms, resulting in contracts being swiftly agreed upon. The end result of this, which was developed and built at Yamaha, but sold as the Toyota 2000 GT, fully met its creators' expectations. Thanks to classical sports-car proportions – which, maybe unintentionally, distract from the Toyota's very compact dimensions – the first racy sports car to come from the Land of the Rising Sun possessed immediate appeal. Then modern features, such as the pop-up headlights, the large, flush glazing of the auxiliary headlights, as well as the more slanted windshield and the tapered side windows, ensured that the Toyota did not come across like a mere Jaguar E-type homage with a few cues referencing Italian coachbuilder Zagato added on top. The light units, as well as their thick chrome trim actually are the clearest indicators as to this sports car's Asian origins. However, the lack of any unnecessary seams on its body acts as a subtle reminder of this Toyota's manufacture pedigree.

In sharp contrast, the 2000 GT's interior clearly conforms to Toyota's archconservative corporate ethos. Apart from two hoods atop the dashboard – one above the instrument gauges, the other placed in front of the passenger, like some kind of symmetrical gimmick – the cockpit is defined by expedience, and the use of exquisite rose wood looks like a

TTQ TOYOTA

Detail of the interior, Toyota 2000 GT, 1967

James Bond, *You Only Live Twice*, 1967, film still

somewhat clumsy, bourgeois attempt at lending the interior an air of dapper sophistication.

In keeping with the Japanese collectivistic culture, the Toyota 2000 GT's main designer was not officially named for years. This allowed a rumour claiming Count Albrecht von Goertz had had a hand in its styling to circulate – but this may now be discounted. For it was Satoru Nozaki, a Toyota in-house stylist, who was eventually named as the design's creator by the company. He had received his assignment in part to also celebrate Toyota's thirty years of car production.

Despite having only been built in very low numbers and barely sold outside of Japan, the Toyota 2000 GT rightfully enjoys an illustrious status. Its unveiling in 1964 coincided with the start of operations of the Tōkaidō Shinkansen (the first Japanese high-speed train) and the Tokyo Olympic Games – all of which acted as strong symbols for the rise of Japan and the country's admission as a member of the Western world. Some years later, the Toyota even succeeded the Aston Martin DB5 in the role of Her Majesty's (as well as cinemagoers' worldwide) favourite spy's preferred means of transportation. Bond's 2000 GT was special insofar as it was a unique roadster version, built in order to accommodate the tall frame of Sean Connery, who played Bond then and who would have hardly fitted inside the coupé.

Rarity, engineering and quality – not to mention its form and pop cultural stature – are what allowed the Toyota 2000 GT to become the first true collector's item among Japanese cars. Which would constitute one more reason for its creator to be proud of.

1 See Jeffrey K. Liker, The Toyota Way, New York 2013, p. 61.

Rear side view of the Toyota 2000 GT, 1967

FERRARI 365 GTB/4 DAYTONA

- DESIGNER LEONARDO FIORAVANTI (B. 1938)
- YEAR 1973, PRODUCED 1969–1973
- PRODUCTION RUN: 1,284 VEHICLES
- 4.4 LITRE CAPACITY, 12 CYLINDERS, 352 HP, MAX SPEED 280 KM/H
- MANUFACTURER: AUTO AVIO COSTRUZIONI FERRARI, MARANELLO
- LENDER: PRIVATE COLLECTION

All over the globe, the year 1968 was characterised by revolutions large and small. One such cataclysm was taking place at Ferrari. Despite being less 'eruptive' than others, it obviously was recognised by the automotive world.

At Modena, a policy of only evolutionary changes to engineering and design had hitherto been pursued, which appeared to stagnate by the end of the 1960s. In this context, the Ferrari 365 GTB/4 – unofficially christened the Daytona – unveiled in that fateful year 1968 may be considered somewhat revolutionary. In terms of engineering, Ferrari may have adhered to the traditional front-engine/rear-wheel-drive layout for the 365 GTB/4, and Carrozzeria Pininfarina was yet again commissioned to come up with the styling. However, the stylists working at Grugliasco, near Turin, had been well aware of what was happening at the same time at Bertone, the avant-garde competitor at that time, just a few miles away. As a consequence, a team of young designers was tasked with lending the Daytona an innovative appearance.

Leonardo Fioravanti was one of these young stylists, and the Daytona would turn out to be the basis of his reputation. Inspired by the milestone BMC-1800/1100 concept cars (British Motor Corporation) his colleague Paolo Martin had previously devised, Fioravanti created the first Ferrari not defined by the hitherto essential soft form language.[1] Apart from its astoundingly even surfaces, it was the characteristic 'graphic' stylistic elements that rendered the Daytona the first Ferrari of a new era. The straight groove running along its side and around the rear certainly constituted both a literal incision and a metaphorical cut with the past, and was only outdone in that regard by the Plexiglass band covering the entire front tip of early Daytonas, which even housed Ferrari's *Cavallino Rampante* emblem. That, in order to accommodate this, the traditionally rounded-off Ferrari grille had to hide deep inside the car's body, flanked by the bumpers, and in the form of a rectangular adaptation, makes this stylistic solution appear all the more bold – and not just by Modenese standards.[2]

Even the said Plexiglass band maintains the kind of graphical clarity that constituted

Detail, front fender, with indicator and light housing, Ferrari 365 GTB/4, 1967

Corvette Stingray, 1969

the Pininfarina standard for many decades. Purely decorative forms are not found on the Daytona, either. Neither does it truly flex its visual muscles – apart from its very masculine track width, that is. The delicate sweep of the bonnet, which is continued in the side window graphics and adapted by the trailing edge at the rear, are all the visual stimulants needed.

It is also due to this expertly handled restraint, when it comes to the dosage of visual excitement applied, that the criticism often levelled at the Daytona – that it looks too 'American' – is ultimately shown up. For despite certain parallels to the Corvette, particularly as far as the basic shape is concerned, the Ferrari appears far more measured, elegant and casual than its New World counterpart.

So all things considered, the Daytona proved to be a big leap for Ferrari design. And one hell of a start for the career of Leonardo Fioravanti. But those were not the only automotive stories written in the year 1968. For in that spring, Giorgetto Giugiaro unveiled his Bizzarrini Manta, before Marcello Gandini presented his Alfa Romeo Carabo in the autumn. The revolution had only just begun.

1 See Leonardo Fioravanti, Il Cavallino Nel Cuore. Autobiography of a Designer, Vimodrone 2015, p. 21; Paolo Martin, Martin's Cars – Pensieri in Tre Dimensioni, Turin 2017, p. 15.
2 See Robert Foskett, Ferrari 308, 328 and 348. The Complete Story, Marlborough 2015, p. 57.

Front view of the Ferrari 365 GTB/4, 1967

FERRARI DINO 246 GTS (TIPO 607 E)

- DESIGNER ALDO BROVARONE (B. 1926)
- YEAR 1973, PRODUCED 1969–1974
- PRODUCTION RUN: 195 VEHICLES
- 2.4 LITRE CAPACITY, 6 CYLINDERS, 193 HP, MAX SPEED 235 KM/H
- MANUFACTURER: AUTO AVIO COSTRUZIONI FERRARI, MARANELLO
- LENDER: COLLECTION DÜSSELDORF

In order to understand the Dino 246 GTS, one must first of all understand what it is not: a Ferrari.

The gospel says that the Dino brand was Enzo Ferrari's homage to his deceased son Alfredino (nicknamed 'Dino'), as the latter had significantly contributed to the V6 engine at the heart of the car that was to bear his name. However, neither of these assumptions is true.

In truth, the Dino brand was created in order to keep Dino, the car, at arm's length from its superior mother, Ferrari. For to that company, a mid-engine layout was deemed as sacrilegious as engines built at Fiat – instead of being assembled by hand at Maranello – and selling prices that were attainable to the merely well-off, rather than to just the obscenely rich.

During the course of the 1960s, Ferrari had started to feel considerable pressure: the Porsche 911 from Stuttgart on the one hand and the shockingly advanced competition coming from Sant'Agata Bolognese in the form of Lamborghini on the other had forced Ferrari's hand. However, the Modenese marque was obviously far too proud to even accept that Ferrari even had any kind of competition at all. Under these circumstances, it hardly comes as a surprise that the impetus for the Dino did not originate from Maranello, but from Ferrari's trusted *carrozzeria*, Pininfarina. There, in Turin, trends and innovations were not blindly ignored, which resulted in the company's young director, Sergio Pininfarina, making it his business to convince *Commendatore* Enzo Ferrari of the merits of both an entry level model and the mid-engined layout.

His success proved Pininfarina right, which he followed by yet another smart decision, when he entrusted the exceedingly capable Aldo Brovarone with the new model's design.[1] Brovarone's fingerprints can be seen all over the Dino 246, be they in the form of the almost feminine kind of elegance the little mid-engined macho machine exudes, in spite of its cheeky flair, or courtesy of the clearly evident aeronautics-inspired details.

Thanks to Brovarone's mastery, the Dino 246's aesthetics also combine what supposedly is contradictory. Therefore soft, almost sinuous curves clad its squat basic packaging. The cabin hunches between enormous, widely spaced wheels, which fill the wheel arches to

Detail, side air vents, Ferrari Dino 246 GTS, 1973

the point where they appear close to bursting. This results in the Dino 246's crouching, but non-aggressive stance, which avoids the usual sports-car clichés. And exactly this was due to Brovarone's assured hand, his penchant for taut, yet soft surfaces, which he tightened across the Dino's frame.[2]

This sense of aplomb also extends to the details. The air vents, semi-encased round headlights or smaller details like the (very small) door handles all add up to a particular impression: the Dino 246 is striking, but never blunt or brash. For it thrills with the intelligence of its body's packaging and the finesse of its styling. And it does so completely without an unending bonnet, a fastback shape or many other contemporary sports-car cues.

At the same time, the Dino also constitutes the last peak of classical sports-car aesthetics before Italian designers Giorgetto Giugiaro and Marcello Gandini proclaimed the wedge shape and sharp edges as the new symbols of performance and speed. In that sense, the Dino 246 was both the pioneer of the mid-engine layout and the swan song to the romantic form language of the post-war era.

Due to this particular significance, the Dino 246's repute exceeds its original status as borderline neglected entry-level model to an almost absurd degree today. But as in many other cases, this constitutes yet another instance of the rebel turning pioneer that eventually led the establishment to admit it to its ranks – after decades of rejection. However, the Dino never was and still is no Ferrari. It is more than that.

1 See Brian Long, Dino. The V6 Ferrari, Dorchester 2015, p. 36.
2 See Giulio Silli, Stile & Raffinatezza, Le Creazioni di Aldo Brovarone, Turin 2015, p. 51.

Front view of the Ferrari Dino 246 GTS, 1973

MERCEDES-BENZ C111 TYP II (CONCEPT CAR)

- DESIGNER BRUNO SACCO (B. 1933)
- PRESENTATION YEAR 1970
- PRODUCTION RUN: 6 VEHICLES
- FOUR-ROTOR WANKEL ENGINE, 350 HP, MAX SPEED 290 KM/H
- MANUFACTURER: DAIMLER-BENZ AG, STUTTGART
- LENDER: MERCEDES-BENZ CLASSIC

In the year 1969, the world of car design was in a half-paralysed, half-manic state. A little earlier, after initial occurrences at lecture theatres and in the streets, a revolt against the constraints of yore and the establishment in general had also seized the automotive realm. This process began in Turin, led by design revolutionaries Giorgetto Giugiaro and Marcello Gandini. Their all-new wedge-shape designs broke with traditional automotive aesthetics and heralded a new era.

In those days, Mercedes-Benz was still very much a company run by men wearing suits, ties and side partings. Despite this, motoring magazines would soon feature spy shots of a somewhat wedge-shaped, gull-winged mid-engined sports car on Stuttgart plates. There was no question about it: 'der Daimler', as the company was referred to in those days, was working on a super car! When it was finally shown to the public in the shape of a series of evolutionary concept vehicles in 1969 and 1970 respectively, this athlete, christened C111, turned out to be a very Swabian, highly engineering-led interpretation of the theme.[1] In fact, the C111 ultimately proved to be more of an anti-super car.

The main difference between the orange Benz and the usual super cars can be traced back to their respective raisons d'être. For the C111 was neither a rich man's toy, nor a stylist's playground. Instead, it was a technology test bed, albeit one featuring gullwing doors. The C111 was intended to embody the pioneering excellence of Swabian engineering through aerodynamic finesse, sophisticated power units, modern composite bodies and a smart chassis. Being good looking was a side effect, at best.

The orange paint, as well as the use of matte black to accentuate certain graphics, not to mention those gullwing doors – which of course are a homage to the already legendary 300 SL – were the only cases of artifice to be found on the C111. Apart from this, the Mercedes appears unquestionably impressive, but at the same time obviously functional. However, some of those functions also served visual purposes: for one, the engineers from Sindelfingen prided themselves on having attained excellent levels of downforce without the kind of spoilers and wings typically necessary to do so.[2] However, in terms of Swabian ostentatious modesty, the restrained

Front view of the Mercedes-Benz C111 Type II, 1970

Section drawing, Mercedes-Benz C111 Type II, 1970

application of air vents is clearly outshone by the almost pietist, demure cabin design, which employs mostly off-the-shelf components. Which comes as a bit of a surprise, given it was an Italian, Bruno Sacco, rather than a Swabian who had been in charge of C111's design. Admittedly, with Vertical Affinity/Horizontal Homogeneity, the same Bruno Sacco would devise the most 'German' car design concept of them all, in the best sense of the term, about a decade later.

Interior apart, the aesthetic ambitions were big enough not to use any other series production parts. Light units and all body parts were exclusive to the C111 – and of a far simpler appearance than the Mercedes production cars of the time, which oscillated between bechromed baroque and technocratic simplicity. From today's perspective, one detail found on the C111 appears particularly astounding in this context: the flying buttresses connecting the roof with the trailing edge. These would be appropriated by Giugiaro on the Maserati Merak a few years later, yet only three decades later did they turn into an industry-wide trend. In that sense, these two buttresses stand for the aerodynamic and design groundwork Mercedes-Benz used to perform on behalf of the entire automotive sector, back in the day. Despite featuring a delicate wedge shape, gullwing doors and a garish paintjob, the C111 therefore constitutes the opposite of the super car as a mere hedonistic exhibit. This, rather than its very low production figure, is what makes it truly unique.

1 See Markus Bolsinger, Design by Mercedes-Benz. Hermann Ahrens, Friedrich Geiger, Bruno Sacco, Peter Pfeiffer, Gorden Wagener, Bielefeld 2008, p. 106.
2 See Wolf-Heinrich Hucho and Syed Rafeeq Ahmed, Aerodynamik des Automobils. Strömungsmechanik, Wärmetechnik, Fahrdynamik, Komfort, Berlin/Heidelberg 2005, p. 464.

Rear side view of the Mercedes-Benz C111 Type II, 1970

BMW TURBO

- DESIGNER PAUL BRACQ (B. 1933)
- PRESENTATION YEAR 1972
- PRODUCTION RUN: 2 VEHICLES
- 2 LITRE CAPACITY, 4 CYLINDERS, 280 HP (TURBOCHARGER), MAX SPEED 250 KM/H
- MANUFACTURER: BAYERISCHE MOTORENWERKE AG, MUNICH
- LENDER: BMW GROUP CLASSIC

The BMW Turbo's relevance is twofold: on the one hand, it was BMW's first ever concept car, on the other hand it also set standards from a cultural perspective.

The BMW Turbo's design in itself offers plenty of talking points. Just as the Mercedes C111 had done two years prior, the BMW adapted the Italian wedge shape as the contemporary cypher for progressiveness. Furthermore, the BMW was also fitted with expressive gullwing doors. Yet all things considered, the Bavarian car was a much more style-conscious effort than its Swabian counterpart, as it was supposed to be a mainly visual statement, whereas the Mercedes served as an engineering test bed and showcase first and foremost. These different emphases manifested themselves in one of the Turbo's most conspicuous details: the covered rear wheels. Depending on which explanation one might prefer to accept, these were either fitted to improve the car's aerodynamics, or where nothing other than a stylistic homage to the pre-war BMW 327 model.

For this reason, one might possibly be led to accuse the BMW Turbo of lacking in substance. However, this would be unfair, certainly as long as aesthetically concerns are at the fore. After all, BMW's then new chief designer, Paul Bracq, had to prove his mettle with the Turbo. The Frenchman had been appointed BMW's design director in 1970 in order to modernise the Bavarian brand both in design terms and structurally, which led to the utmost importance being placed on the Turbo concept car. To everyone's relief, the sports car, what with its planar body (initially without the rear wheel spats fitted and plain coloured), lived up to this expectation. Whereas the simultaneously unveiled BMW 5 series saloon was obviously still rooted in the 1960s in terms of proportions and form language, the Turbo was all about modernism. Shiny metal or chrome are found only on the wheels, the badges and around the BMW emblem. But everywhere else, clean, black, cutting-edge, industrial design-inspired graphics reign supreme, as they not so much disguise the creases separating different parts of the body from one another, as highlight them.

Particularly in terms of consistency, this approach was similar to what was done at Porsche in those days, where the most

BMW Turbo in front of the Olympiastadion, Munich, 1972

Paul Braqc (l.) and Giovanni Michelotti (m.) in front of a wood mock-up of the BMW Turbo, ca. 1971

modern design of any German car maker was not just conceived, but even put into production. However, as far as BMW production cars were concerned, the Turbo remained mostly ephemeral – if it was not for the M1 sports car unveiled in 1978, for which Giugiaro had deliberately used the Turbo as a source of inspiration. Another car showcasing a graphical approach similar to the Turbo's would eventually go into production about twenty years later, in the form of the Klaus Kapitza-designed BMW 8 series coupé.

In actual fact, the BMW Turbo's distinctiveness exceeds its value to the automotive realm, for it played a part in the equally innovative and progressive self-projection of the city of Munich during the Olympic Games in the summer of 1972.[1] Those 'colourful games' were supposed both to matter in terms of athletic and commercial issues, and also to focus on the economic re-emergence of West Germany. For that reason, Günther Behnisch's 'democratic sports facilities' at Olympiapark were accompanied not only by Otl Aicher's groundbreaking pictograms,[2] but also – just across the busy Petuelring Road – by Karl Schwanzer's 'Vierzylinder' high-rise office block, BMW's new corporate headquarters. As well as Paul Bracq's BMW Turbo, of course.

The parallels between Aicher's graphics, Schwanzer's façade grid and Bracq's segmentation of the Turbo's body do not end with common stylistic devices like the rounded-off edges ('squircles') or the stringent alignment of lines, which could also be found on the contemporary designs of Dieter Rams. Indeed, all of this was a topical update of the Ulmer Schule's concept of 'gute Form' – even though nobody really cared about that, back in 1972.

1 See Tony Lewin, The Complete Book of BMW, Minneapolis, MN, 2004, p. 308.
2 See Otl Aicher, Die Welt als Entwurf, Berlin 1991, p. 153.
3 See Anne Bracklow, Markenarchitektur in der Konsumwelt. Branding zur Distinktion, Heidelberg 2004, p. 173.

Front view with open gullwing doors, BMW Turbo, 1972

LANCIA STRATOS HF

- DESIGNER MARCELLO GANDINI (B. 1938)
- YEAR 1976, PRODUCED 1973–1978
- PRODUCTION RUN: APP. 495 VEHICLES
- 2.4 LITRE CAPACITY, 6 CYLINDERS, 195 HP, MAX SPEED 248 KM/H
- MANUFACTURER: LANCIA & C., TURIN
- LENDER: SCUDERIA TREDICI MONACI

When form and function turn out equally innovative, one can justifiably speak of a milestone. As in the case of the Lancia Stratos.

The groundbreaking combination of sports and rally car played with conventions – or outright broke them. On the Stratos, the wedge shape is therefore combined with increased ride height, and extreme compactness with dynamic forms. Due to its immense visual presence, the Stratos could easily be taken for a mainly aesthetic statement *à la* Lamborghini Countach. Yet the Lancia possessed a clear function, one which it fulfilled with aplomb – as proven by its myriad rally successes.

The basic shape of the Stratos is of astonishing sculptural clarity: a double wedge whose pronunciation varies. On the flanks, it is more understated, whereas it tapers in more extreme a fashion at the front – in conjunction with the visor-like windscreen. Massive wheelhouses, which almost appear to 'rupture' the front wings, break through the wedge shape. The end result of this is a most expressive body shape of the kind that is usually found among concept cars, but hardly on a production vehicle.

Each and every detail of the Stratos is of geometric consistency, which must not be mistaken for simplicity, though. The round rear lights, headlights and door handles may have been taken from mass-market models, yet in the context of the Lancia they appear like precious industrial design items. The air vents on the bonnet and the rear hatch's dramatic opening mechanism are unashamedly grand gestures, delivered with typically Italian verve.

Despite all this, one must not forget quite how compact the Stratos really is. Its extremely short, rally-prepared wheelbase defines a body of, by today's standards, almost absurd compactness. The ensuing inconsistency between its contained physical dimensions and its potent flair is what defines the Lancia's appeal.

The Lancia Stratos' reported origin story appears unusual well. Legend has it that Nuccio Bertone, owner of the *carrozzeria* of the same name, was extremely keen on expanding business with Lancia, which led him to assign his chief designer, Marcello Gandini, to create a truly extreme, Lancia-based concept car

BERTONE
HF

Detail of the rear of the Lancia Stratos HF, 1976

Front view of the Lancia Stratos HF, 1976

by the name of the Stratos Zero. In order to present the finished, truly mad Stratos Zero to Lancia's management, Bertone himself allegedly drove the car through the main entrance at Lancia's Borgo San Paolo factory – under the barrier, thanks to the Stratos Zero's extremely low body. Equally impressed with Bertone's chutzpa and the Stratos Zero's design, Lancia management then agreed to the construction of yet another prototype.[1]

This is the legend, which may be disputed. What's free of doubt, though, is that the Stratos, as it was first unveiled in Gandini-penned[2] concept-car guise in 1971, constituted yet another case-in-point for Bertone's boundless creativity during those years. It clearly demonstrated the company's then current style, yet once more added new nuances to it too.

When looking at Gandini's entire oeuvre, though, it becomes clear that the sensational Stratos not only embodied a number of the qualities that stood for Gandini at his creative peak, but that it also, ever so discreetly, ushered in the late phase of the designer's work at Bertone. In that sense, the Lancia not only features the vigorous, yet fleet-footed finesse of Gandini's early designs, it is also the first sign of his future penchant for a boldly geometrical form language, which would eventually result in blocky designs of the likes of the Lancia Sibilo and Ferrari Rainbow.

In the case of the Stratos, this tendency meant nothing other than yet another facet of a new, fresh, enchanting automotive design. Or, in other words: a true milestone car.

1 Graham Robson, Lancia Stratos: Rallye Giants, Poundbury 2007, p. 22
2 Gautam Sen, Marcello Gandini – Maestro of Design, vol. 1, Deerfield 2017, p. 212

Side view with boot and bonnet open, Lancia Stratos HF, 1976

LAMBORGHINI COUNTACH 5000 QV

- DESIGNER MARCELLO GANDINI (B. 1938)
- YEAR 1986, PRODUCED 1974–1990
- PRODUCTION RUN: 610 VEHICLES
- 5.2 LITRE CAPACITY, 12 CYLINDERS, 455 HP, MAX SPEED 295 KM/H
- MANUFACTURER: NUOVA AUTOMOBILI FERRUCCIO LAMBORGHINI SPA, SANT'AGATA BOLOGNESE
- LENDER: PRIVATE COLLECTION

Even revolutionaries eventually tire, get comfortable or just grow old. When the Lamborghini Countach was first shown to an astounded public in 1971 in concept car form, it was one of the most radical representatives of the recently invented wedge shape. It went into series production in 1974, named the Countach LP400, and instantly made almost any other automotive devices appear aesthetically compromised.

To dedicate – or even subordinate – a production automobile to a particular stylistic idea in as radical a fashion as Lamborghini had done was simply outrageous. And at the same time hardly surprising, given the Ferrari challenger from Sant'Agata Bolognese and Bertone of Turin had already repeatedly, and with quite some relish, broken with the conventions of automotive design before. The LP400's appearance accordingly turned out utterly brazen and had no competition to fear in terms of 'wedginess' whatsoever, apart maybe from Giugiaro's far more delicate Lotus Esprit.[1]

Styled by Bertone chief designer Marcello Gandini at the peak of his abilities, the Countach LP400 constituted a bona fide provocation.[2] Brutally flat and featuring ludicrous scissor doors, it rendered almost any other car, if not banal than certainly inconsistent. And yet Gandini's form was no mere grandstanding effort, but quite refined. The discreet kink of the razor-sharp edge running alongside the Countach's flanks, as well as the asymmetrical rear wheel arch – which would eventually become a somewhat contrived Gandini trademark – lend the Lamborghini just about enough verve for a subliminal whiff of elegance to emerge, amidst all that ostentatious edginess. Exactly this hint of grace, which the Countach LP400 ever so delicately exudes, was getting lost with each successive model generation though. For as aesthetically consistent and definite as the early Countach may appear, as compromised was it as a production automobile.

For that reason, but also due to the emerging 'if you've got it, flaunt it' *zeitgeist* of the 1980s, the Countach successively started to lose any sense of subtlety from 1978 onwards. This process began with the extension of its wheel arches, which was necessitated by the fitting of extra-wide tyres (onto sensational

Lamborghini Countach 25°Anniversario, 1990

Lamborghini Countach LP400, 1974

Detail of the bonnet, Lamborghini Countach 5000 QV

Campagnolo *Bravo* rims). It was continued through the addition of a massive rear wing, which not merely promised, but actually succeeded at improving the car's high-speed stability - although many Countach owners fitted it on the basis of debatable aesthetic motives. A lid here, a spoiler or air vent there, or maybe some golden accents on top: with each passing year, the Countach became more opulent, plump and heavy-handed – in every regard. This was not just due to advances in engineering, but also because of the increasingly popular aesthetic of rowdy-car tuning that would become a trademark of 1980s automotive culture. The ageing Countach did not elude this trend – on the contrary, it actually found itself spearheading it.

This devolution eventually came to an (un)worthy close with the 25th Anniversary Countach. To celebrate its maker's jubilee, it gained not just smoothed, body-coloured addenda, but also latticed air intakes – in a style very similar to the Modenese competition's form language. These contemporary changes finally made the erstwhile revolutionary look truly old.

No form remains new forever. No revolution lasts forever. No design is perfect. The fate of the Countach is therefore neither surprising nor particularly lamentable. On top of this, is also symbolically stands for the creative history of its creator – for Gandini never again came up with a design as powerful as the LP400's.

1 See Peter Vann, Design by Giugiaro, Stuttgart 2003, p. 111.
2 See Gautam Sen, Marcello Gandini – Maestro of Design, vol. 2, Deerfield, IL, 2017, p. 41.

Front view with open scissor doors, Lamborghini Countach 5000 QV, 1986

SPORTS-CAR DESIGN – THE SHAPE OF SPEED

MARKUS CASPERS

Though when seen in retrospect history presents itself as a linear sequence, it is in fact messy, one thing on top of another, a collection of events not happening at the same time, of delays, accelerations and layers. The same is true of design. The extreme rupture that World War Two was for the twentieth century influenced the development of automobile design from 1950 onwards in two ways: there were references to pre-war trends on the one hand, and longed-for modernity on the other hand. So that by the end of the 1950s we can discern both the formal language of the American streamline design and also the aerodynamic form of the 1930s. At the same time, on both sides of the Atlantic new styles were being created that were initiated by the distinctive Scuola Italiana, whose impact can be traced to the 1960s.

BODYWORK

It was only around 1940 that the automotive form 'found itself', meaning that it rid itself of some of the features that had served as inspirations for the design of the car body up until then: horse-drawn carriages, railway coaches, ships, torpedoes and aeroplanes. Chrysler's Thunderbolt concept car (1941, Alex Tremulis) [Fig. 1] and the specialist auto bodies by Pininfarina and Anderloni/Touring for Mille-Miglia racing cars in 1939 and 1940 are considered the first examples of the ponton style, meaning that the fenders that were previously considered indispensable were dispensed with or integrated into an uninterrupted side panel. But it was only in the late 1950s that it was possible to put the ponton style into mass production. This should be kept in mind when looking at legendary automobiles of the time, many of which are still in the style of the pre-war period, such as the Jaguar XK 120 or the BMW 502, as well as the Delahayes and Bentleys, to name but a few. The Porsche 356 follows the organic flow of pre-war aerodynamic design just like the Mercedes 300 SL racing car of 1952, the inspiration for the road version. In this context, the design of the Cisitalia, introduced in 1946, must have seemed hypermodern. Pininfarina later adapted this basic shape for various brands and models (a standard practice in the Italian *carrozzerias*) and continued to develop it for Ferrari until the early 1960s. [Fig. 2] Early publications on automobile design – often called 'styling' until the 1980s – expressed the idea that automotive form followed a process of evolution that would one day be completed: the geometric 'functional form' based on the wedge shape was the final stage in this development – the car was now

Fig. 1: The ponton style: Chrysler Thunderbolt, Ralph Roberts, Alex Tremulis, 1941
Fig. 2: The basic design of a slim European sport coupé: Fiat 1100 ES, Battista 'Pinin' Farina, 1950

grown-up and sensible. This style, for which Giorgetto Giugiaro's studio ItalDesign was pioneering, claimed every genre globally from 1975 onwards, from compact cars to family saloons, from high-end limousines to sports cars. We now know that things did not turn out like that, and that the era of faceless Euro-cars was followed by a wave of retro designs and the return of biomorphic or at least organically soft contours (and much more). So, back to the beginning?

FORM AND FUNCTION

Form follows many things, not only function. One of the biggest misunderstandings in design is based on the dichotomy of form and function. Both form and function are in most cases ill-founded or not understood. In Germany in particular, there is still a crude understanding of design which is based on a historically precarious notion of form and function. The mantra of 'form follows function'[1] repeated ad infinitum dates back to a time when goods fashioned by hand were pushed aside by those fabricated industrially, and this new type of 'product' had to assert itself against competitors with justifications, including aesthetic ones. It is beyond question that pliers have to be shaped the way they are so they can grip, pull, pinch and cut. Things are different, however, when it comes to radios, lamps and cars (not to mention electronic and digital systems). There is no longer any form that needs to follow function. A car will drive regardless of whether it is shaped like a shoe box or an aerofoil. As

Fig. 3: GM Motorama 1954, a roadshow exhibiting concept cars and production models that was met with great enthusiasm in the United States throughout the 1950s

Fig. 4: Chrysler D'Elegance, Virgil Exner, 1952

we know today, however, it will drive better if aerodynamic considerations have been taken into account. For that reason, the right angle of the functionalists from the Bauhaus or the Hochschule für Gestaltung in Ulm was never concerned with locomotion (the only things the latter institution produced in the field of transport design were tractors, road rollers and commuter trains – boxes, basically). The functions of the automobile we have been working with since around 1928 are only partially utilitarian these days (this could be represented by a tool character and a corresponding utility value); they are primarily social *functives.* With the onset of industrial design, form has always also been charged both semiotically and socially: the form of objects symbolise their use and they become signs (in the semiotic sense).[2] We can lament the loss of the historical utility value (and believe 'the good old things' still exist), but the beginning of automobile design on an industrial scale, as brought about by Harley Earl at General Motors in 1928, marks a paradigm shift for the entire field of design history and theory. Car manufacturers and their designers were the first to understand what design means. Besides the necessary cladding of the technical components, it largely concentrates on the aesthetic expression of societal ideas, whether focused on the future or the past, whether functional or sensual, and whether aimed at status or understatement. [Fig. 3] This is the only way to perceive the large variety, the lack of concurrence and the contradictions in product design that we witnessed during the 'golden age' of automobile design between 1950 and 1980. During these decades, there was just one ideological and aesthetic direction: forwards to the future, both technologically and aesthetically. However, the forms of this conceived modernity varied. Many manufacturers would have loved to be a part of this, but they simply lacked the finance for new product/design developments. This explains the longevity of many designs and models, such as the Jaguar E-type and the Porsche 911. Captivating as we might find both today, in 1977 their design, which went back to the late 1950s/early 1960s, was already dated. The social and aesthetic mainstream saw the future in the wedge shape, in garishly coloured plastic bodies, gullwing doors and alloy rims. These temporal dislocations – caused by the much longer development times needed, by today's standards, for new models, as well as by the above-mentioned financial limitation – mean that we perceive the automotive streetscape of earlier decades as more diverse and varied than today's.

BETWEEN DETROIT AND TURIN

None of the European sports-car manufacturers would have survived without the American market; many Italian design studios would also have had to shut up shop without the collaboration with one of the major American companies (there were still four or five in the 1950s and 1960s). As a result, it is not surprising that the Detroit Style and the Scuola Italiana greatly influenced each other. [Fig. 4] At first glance, the chrome-loving limousines of the rocket era seem to have nothing in common with the slim sports machines designed in Turin, but details such as panoramic windscreens and rear lights with the gunfire look confirm mutual inspiration. Ghia worked intensively with and for Chrysler, Pininfarina for Frazer Nash and General Motors. The chief designers at General Motors, Chrysler and Ford regularly visited automobile fairs in Paris, London and Geneva in order to learn about new stylistic developments and to recruit talented designers. While comfort and opulence were associated with American limousines, European sports cars stood for athleticism, speed and streamlined bodies. Max Hoffman, a car importer who fled Austria to escape the Nazis, first made the success of many European sports cars possible in the United States in the 1950s: with the Jaguar XK 120, the Porsche 356, the Mercedes 300 SL, the BMW 507 and the Alfa Romeo Giulia Spider, it was Hoffman who either triggered production runs by pre-ordering cars, made suggestions for new models (Porsche 356 Speedster, BMW 507), or introduced manufacturers to the right designers (such as Count Albrecht von Goertz and BMW).

The evolution of the form of a design largely follows social and economic motivations that aim at distinctiveness – at social and cultural differentiation from neighbours on the one hand, and at competitive advantages over others in the market on the other. The stylistic shift away from the flamboyant, over-the-top rocket design with oversize rear fins and panoramic windows towards basic geometric shapes occurred between 1959 and 1961 in the United States. In Europe, meanwhile, the trapezoid shape was replacing the soft ponton forms with embryonic fenders on limousines, while sports-car design often remained loyal to the biomorphic, aerodynamic lines of the 1950s. It was only in the mid-1960s that American formal design such as 'Coke-bottle styling' (which was in turn influenced by European sports cars) became combined with concepts from racing-car construction to produce a new supercar look. The Bizzarini GT and the Lamborghini Miura are good examples, their designs representing the transition from organic flow to geometric wedge. Until this point, we could talk about

Fig. 5: The high point of the formalised wedge shape: Lancia Sibilo, Marcello Gandini (for Bertone), 1978

Fig. 6: Nuccio Bertone in front of Marcello Gandini's Alfa Romeo Carabo, 1968

a traceable development, if we accept that the 'wedge' was somehow an ideal form to which everything led. But even that would be only part of the truth, as the Italian design studios were vigorously competing with each other. Since Pininfarina largely remained loyal to the soft, flowing style, from 1968 onwards Bertone started countering its great competitor with radical, emblematically geometric designs. [Fig. 5] While Ghia, Michelotti and Frua preferred an understated modern style, sometimes inspired by US designs, Pininfarina and Bertone implemented their own 'corporate design', regardless of who the client was. Citroën, Volvo, Fiat, Lancia and Lamborghini had faith in Bertone and trusted that the manufacturer's logo would be enough of a distinguishing factor for buyers. Austin in Britain, Peugeot in France, and Lancia and Ferrari in Italy hired Pininfarina for decades, and in the 1960s had no problem with the fact that the fronts of their vehicles with the typical grille and corresponding headlight positions were signatures of the design studio rather than embodiments of the identity of their own brands.

THE FORM OF IDEAS

In addition to stylistic demarcations within the industry, there was also a major ideological debate surrounding the form of objects between 1955 and 1970. American design was referred to as 'styling' in Europe and that was certainly meant in a pejorative sense. The spearhead of this styling were the American automobiles that displayed annual design changes without at the same time delivering new utility value in the form of technical innovations – hence the accusation. European designers tried to counter this styling practice with a design ethic that drew on the ideas of 1920s functionalism. The renaissance of rationalism in design had become an influential idea at various institutions in the 1950s: at the Hochschule für Gestaltung (University of Design) in Ulm, in Swiss typography, at the Rat für Formgebung (German Design Council) in Germany, the Ausschuss 'Gute Form' ('Good Form' Committee) in Switzerland, and the 'Good Design' label – they all helped promote the idea that geometric shapes, avoiding irregularly shaped curves and cambered surfaces, are rational and functional, that they are inherently stable designs that counter the short-lived, fashionable wow factor.[3] As a result, it could happen that an angular car body was considered more 'rational' in 1963 than a flowing one, even if the former had a poor drag coefficient. However, attributes such as stylish, modern, trendy and so on are not associated with specific forms; instead, they vary with the aesthetic ideas of a certain cultural era. The motorised irrationality known as the sports car had at least to exhibit a rational body form in Germany – and maybe that also contributed to the popularity of the 911 design.

Form conveys meaning, ideas; that's unavoidable. A design can attempt to communicate speed, athleticism and strength through form alone, so that a car may look fast even when stationary and when the actual performance numbers do not support the claim. This was the accusation hurled at many medium-sized sports cars between 1968 and 1980, such as the Opel GT: they looked great, but had unexciting mass-production technology under their bonnets.

FORM AND TIME

Objects help us to orient ourselves in time. We associate forms with memories – our own and those we borrow; memories of times that we mostly think of as good and wonderful because we experienced, coped with and secured the past. This function of remembering is expressed in aesthetics. The fact that we are today fascinated by Gandini's designs is based on the fact that they are historical, even though we still sense their avant-garde or futuristic impetus. However, would we be able to say, hand on heart, that we would have swooned over Gandini's Carabo concept car for Alfa Romeo at the Paris Motor Show in 1968? [Fig. 6] Would we not have liked to take our bearings from the form repertoire that was already secured at the time, and preferred the Lamborghini Miura, which was released two years earlier? We associate life experiences with forms – if we evaluate these experiences as positive, we are more likely to think of the forms as 'good'. This life experience is largely transmitted through the mass media today: films, books, posters, photos and digital media bring pop culture into our lives. We never see a form as isolated and without context; so we associate sports cars with the Roman *dolce vita* of the early 1960s, the era of the jet set on the Côte d'Azur or with the London of the Swinging Sixties – even though these attributions are sometimes based on media distortions. The Jaguar E-type, for example, was not a car driven by the English pop aristocracy (they drove Bentleys, Aston Martins and Mini Coopers); in 1965, an E-type was more likely to be parked outside the Whisky a Go Go in Los Angeles.[4]

The fact that design is a reflection of its time is both true and trite. This has been accepted for almost every area of design. And more than that: research is carried out, classifications established, exhibitions organised, publications issued, and a cult around the creators generated. In this respect, it is automobile design that leads a life in the shadows, remaining a field for nerds and geeks. It is outshone by a fetish for the different marques and is dismissed as transient fashion. No other area of design has shaped our streetscene, the image of societies, cultures and periods of time as much as the car has. But there is hardly a designed product produced in such numbers as an automobile (has anyone ever heard of the five millionth Wassily Chair?), and who knows whether, while someone is casually leafing through a magazine sitting in an Eames Lounge Chair, there is a Hickman or a Porsche Lapine outside the door? If we were to live in a world full of 'classic' cars it would be unbearable, because the allegedly timeless design of one object or another stops time, makes it stand still: that is death. The accusation levelled at certain designs in general and at car design in particular – namely that it is fleeting, ephemeral and superficial – is just a reflection of ourselves. Design has the remit and the power to translate our ideas, dreams and desires into forms – we just have to have the ideas first.

1 Though architect Louis Sullivan from Chicago used the formula in an essay in 1896, it was coined in 1815 by the French zoologist and palaeontologist Georges Cuvier, who used it in regard to his research on dinosaurs.
2 We largely owe these insights to Roland Barthes and Umberto Eco, who dedicated themselves to semiological analysis from the 1960s onwards, as well as to the sociologist Pierre Bourdieu, who in *Distinction* (1978) developed a theory of the socially effective symbolism of design using French automobiles and their owners as examples.
3 Wilhelm Braun-Feldweg, 'Amerikanisches, allzu Amerikanisches ...', in: Beiträge zur Formgebung, Essen 1960.
4 See Markus Caspers, Pop. Eine Einführung, Cologne 2011.

PUT THAT THING IN SPORT

PAOLO TUMMINELLI

RELEVANCE

There is an urgent need to explain sports cars to the generation born in a closed Scénic (1996) and raised in a Tiguan (2007) that is brimming over with airbags and driver-assist tools and that has internalised the automobile as belted cruise control. The words of Henry Ford are still pertinent: 'At first the "horseless carriage" was considered merely a freak notion and many wise people explained with particularity why it could never be more than a toy. [...] When it was found that an automobile really could go and several makers started to put out cars, the immediate query was as to which would go fastest. It was a curious but natural development – that racing idea. I never thought anything of racing, but the public refused to consider the automobile in any light other than a fast toy. Therefore later we had to race.'[1] As a result, the automobile became a story of speed that can be explained only by invoking the urge for the irrational that has shaped humankind since time immemorial. The automobile became an expression of potency. Pure masculinity. Image cultivation. Brutal competition. Winner takes all. Ford even suggests that without sports cars there would be no cars. And indeed in the design context everything is connected. Wilhelm Maybach's first Mercedes (1902) was born as a racing car, but at the same time provided the foundation of the modern automobile. [Fig. 1] Alex Issigonis's first offering was an open single-seater, inspired by German grand-prix racers, called the Lightweight Special (1938); his greatest was the Mini (1959) – a pop icon, a successful sports car and an intelligent 'matchbox' all in one. Not least, 'Ferry' Porsche issued the following prediction on his 75th birthday: 'The last car to be built will be a sports car.'[2]

DRAWING A LINE

Impossible. The line separating sports cars and racing cars is blurred. It was not uncommon for 'street legal' versions of thoroughbred competition cars to be offered for official homologation; the Lancia Stratos (1973) is one example. Intoxicated by speed, people did not shy away from using Topolinos – the tiny mouse-nosed Fiats (1936) – and Isabellas – the smart Borgward limousines (1954) – in motor sports. In America, 'stock car' is synonymous with racing car. In line with the motto 'race on Sunday, sell on Monday', increasingly elaborate technical and aesthetic modifications were used to transform even sluggish family carriages into loud so-called 'touring cars'. The line becomes even more blurred when we look at the high-performance 'muscle car' (1960s) or the GTI phenomenon (1980s) that derived from all this: with a little

Fig. 1: Gordon Bennet Cup, 2 July 1903, winner Camille Jenatzy with the Mercedes Simplex 60hp

bit of tuning and a lot of marketing, production models were pimped up to become wannabe sports cars. That's why sports cars can be big or small, open or closed, rounded or angular, and offer an optional number of seats and doors. Nevertheless – and herein lies the magic – a true sports car is immediately recognisable. In the fast lane on the highway, in the supermarket car park, while cruising on a bypass: its most important visual attribute is its emphatically low-lying nature – regardless of whether this is the unique Ford GT40 (1963) [Fig. 2], which gets its name from its height of 40 inches – a metre more or less – or all the lowered Opel Mantas (from 1970). Such a crouched position strongly contradicts the notion of an upright posture and instead generates untameable animalistic behaviour. Never mind its overall form, every sports car is low to the ground and the sexual connotation is unmistakable. When animals hunt they run in a ducked position – images we would have to invent if they did not already exist. The low-lying appearance implies a natural symbiosis between the car and the road. Everything flows, rubs and merges aesthetically. And in doing so raises itself to heavenly heights. This explains how an object that requires minimum mass can create the maximum aesthetic effect.

GENDER

Jim Douglas, the racing driver in Disney's family comedy *The Love Bug* (1968), puts it in a nutshell: 'Without the right car, I am half the man.' The young woman by his side smiles devotedly. A widespread cliché naturally associates sports cars with male machismo! In fact, it was Fascism that created the narrative of the powerful car as a potency device for the little man. The racing car was a propaganda machine, its driver a hero, ready to take off, to break records – such as the unfortunate Bernd Rosemeyer, who died at the wheel of his Auto Union racer in 1938. And it was not just countless racing-car drivers who died for the immortality of the automobile. In 1955, aged just twenty-four, the Hollywood star and young rebel James Dean destroyed his Porsche 550 Spyder in a collision with a middle-class Ford, making driving a sports car a very cool thing to do and turning the 'Made in Zuffenhausen' into 'hot wheels'. In 1970, Janis Joplin jeered 'my friends all drive Porsches' and asked the Lord to buy her a Mercedes-Benz. Joplin actually drove a Porsche 356 C convertible (1964) featuring a hand-painted psychedelic livery. In 'Motorsport' (2018), the rapper Nicki Minaj insisted: 'Put that thing in sport', asking 'Why would I hop in some beef (why?) / When I could just hop in a Porsche?', while boasting, 'I can actually afford to get a pink Bugatti'. In fact, the rapper drives a Porsche and a Lamborghini and a Bentley and ... many others, all brand new and invariably pink. With her buying power, Nicki Minaj confirms a trend: more and more women are driving luxury sports cars. In Asia, they have become the most important target group for Ferrari & co. Irrespective of its performance, acquiring a sports car is as much a given to them as wearing a fashion accessory, and they like to display them nonchalantly while going at no more than a brisk jog. Nothing new is invented; instead, a wilted fig leaf is finally removed. At the age of twenty-one, the French writer Françoise Sagan totalled her Aston Martin DB 2/4 (1957) – going at 180 km/h, mind – and miraculously survived the rollover. As a result, she did not replicate Dean's fatal career move and so failed to become a legend. Still more: Tamara de Lempicka drove a Bugatti, Ingrid Bergman a Ferrari, Gae Aulenti a Porsche. Artist Sylvie Fleury's very first car was a Camaro. When she was denied entry to a muscle car club, she set up her own. Thereafter, the cult film *She-Devils on Wheels* (1968) mutated into her own artistic performance (1997). Art meets car meets culture. The Italian popular hero Gabriele D'Annunzio, who, depending on one's point of view, can be seen as poet, war hero or playboy, asserted that 'the car is female' (1926) – surely meaning the sports car.

Fig. 2: Ford GT40, Eric Broadley, John Wyer, 1963–1968

VINTAGE

In the early days, the appeal of the sports car was largely performance. The belief was that a bigger engine was all that was needed. Brakes were rarely fitted. Sports cars were aimed at customers who took part in motor sports, those who owned such vehicles for fun, and those who raced them for money. With the exception of the experimental teardrop shape that became fashionable in the 1930s, and was often used for breaking records, not much attention was given to the body. It was almost as if sports cars consisted largely of a bonnet on wheels. Weight was not the only reason for dispensing with a metal roof. The competition was direct, the race literally head-to-head. [Fig. 3] It was vital for drivers that they were able to see and move. Splendidly dangerous, the whole thing! The trend for sporty luxury cars developed over time. Basically, the first supercars were exotic, exclusive and hardly practical. This category included masterpieces such as the Bugatti T57 (1934–1940), the Alfa Romeo models 8C 2300 and 2900 (1931–1939), and the Mercedes-Benz K series (W29, 1934–1939). Although legendary now, these cars were as rare as hen's teeth when they were made. Over a total of twenty-two production years, the combined total for all three models was no more than 1,800 vehicles. Even the BMW 328 (1937), a very successful, and at 7,400 reichsmarks a relatively affordable, open-top vehicle – the Mercedes-Benz 540 K cost 28,000 reichsmarks at the time – saw a production run of just 500 over a period of three years.

Fig. 3: Benito Mussolini in an Alfa Romeo P3 2600, 1932

The Jaguar XK120 (1948) created a new self-image for the whole category. William Lyons' lovely creation, whose name hinted at the then incredible top speed of 120 miles per hour, was not just the most powerful and fastest car in the world, it was also an affordable beauty suitable for everyday use, one that a 'gentleman driver' could drive to the office in the morning, to the opera in the evening and on the racetrack at the weekend, all the while looking great. For seven days Stirling Moss and three others drove the Fixed-Head Coupé (1951) in Monthléry at more than 160 kilometres per hour. Disc brakes were trialled at Le Mans (1953). Hollywood star Clark Gable drove an XK, his fellow actor Humphrey Bogart had the press take pictures of him by a Jag, together with Lauren Bacall and their son Stephen in front of their villa in Beverly Hills. Success was guaranteed: in seven years, 12,045 XK120 models were produced, 85 per cent of them intended for export. With the arrival of the Jaguar, the sports car mutated from an engineering extravagance into an economic and social phenomenon.

IDEAL

The Jaguar XK embodied the ideal of a classic roadster. The engine, fitted longitudinally behind the front axle, resulted in an extra-long bonnet; the sweeping door line – designed to give the helmsman more elbow space – emphasises both the driver, who sits almost on the back wheel, and the fender, which features a bold curve that creates the impression of a short, pert derrière. Its curves and sensuality are almost impossible to beat. The combination of man and machine forces us to interpret the elongated vehicle as a phallus – what an icon! This successful design code was adopted and enhanced further by the BMW 507 (1956), the Ferrari 250 GT Spyder California (1957) and, above all, by the Jaguar E-type (1961) – the sensuous became frankly erotic.

The Cisitalia 202 (1947), designed by Giovanni Savonuzzi and built by Pininfarina, is seen as the inspiration for classic sports cars. [Fig. 4] Its fame lies largely in the fact that Philip Johnson presented it as one of '8 automobiles' at the famous exhibition of that name at MoMA in New York (1951) – installed as a 'rolling sculpture' on a marble roadway. Among the other vehicles on display were a pre-war

MG and a military Jeep. Cisitalia's creator, Piero Dusio, had the vision of building a small but mighty sports car based on popular mechanics, a vision that 'Ferry' Porsche would later successfully implement. The result is remarkable in two ways. The small, closed body, branded 'Berlinetta' by 'Pinin' Farina, gave the two-seater protection from the elements and good levels of comfort, visibility and safety. It therefore had a high utility value, which was to secure its commercial success. In order to meet Dusio's brief, Farina integrated a horizontally elongated grille in the American style, just as Harley Earl had done for the Buick Y-Job (1938). Only the flat bonnet that sat deep between the fenders was really innovative. The decision to maintain the traditional curve of the hips and the sporting proportions – a long bonnet, compact roof, short rear – resulted in a formative style and an elegant vehicle. This design concept found its most successful adaptations in the Ferrari 250 GT SWB ('short wheel base'; 1959) and the Aston Martin DB4 GT by Zagato (1960). This example is rooted so firmly in legend that a remarkable continuity was to be observed during a revival of classic design in the new millennium. One example is the Aston Martin DB9 (2004), the first model of the VH (vertical/horizontal) architecture introduced by Ulrich Bez, another is the BMW Z4 Coupé (2006), the apotheosis of Chris Bangle's 'flame surfacing'.

Fig. 4: Cisitalia 202, drawing, 1947

HYPERBOLE

Stranded on Earth as if from a distant planet: the first genuine work by Marcello Gandini for Bertone was the Lamborghini Marzal (1967). The skin was faceted, metallic and transparent, the 'face' was covered by a dark narrow slit. Gandini's second shot was the Carabo (1968) [Fig. 5], a green prototype based on the Alfa Romeo 33 racing car.

It was thanks to this vehicle that mid-engine construction found its final form: a radically erased face, a flat bonnet with no transition to the windscreen, and the visual weight completely shifted to the rear. Such was the wedge shape: a radical rearrangement of the principles of automobile aesthetics that had held true until then. There were technical and symbolic reasons behind the wedge. With increasing speeds, the classic streamline quickly reached its limit: the automobile took off. In order to counter this lift, efforts were made in the early 1960s to equip racing cars with rear spoilers; Chaparral's Can-Am racing car (1966) turned something that had literally 'spoilt' the style into an icon. Combined with the mid-engine, which challenged automobile designers to rethink the classic design canon, it seemed like a sensible idea to view the entire rear of a car as a spoiler. In order to produce downforce, the back end was raised up, which meant that the engineless front could come closer to the ground – thus necessarily creating the wedge shape. In fact, aerodynamically the wedge was only marginally more efficient than the teardrop; however, it made it possible for enormous forces to be purposefully unleashed close to the ground.

Fig. 5: Presentation of the Alfa Romeo Carabo, Marcello Gandini, 1968

At the same time, it symbolised the ultimate victory of the shape: an emblem of man's control over the undesirable phenomena of nature. The symbolism of a driver seated in front of the engine and displayed as if in a shop window is unmistakeable. The Carabo unleashed a design competition: Giugiaro's Bizzarrini Manta (1968), the Mercedes-Benz C111 (1969), Pininfarina's Ferrari 512 S Modulo (1970) and BMW's Turbo (1971). In 1971, Bertone announced the Countach. Its sleek profile is forced into a geometric frame: Gandini's Lamborghini is a radical hyperbole of style, an aesthetic elemental force that challenges driver and beholder alike. Not a car for the road but a machine for hyperspace. Its theoretical top speed: 315 kilometres per hour. The Countach sentenced the classic automobile shape to death, and in doing so became the ultimate icon. The sports car as UFO. Not just every Lamborghini but every mid-engine supercar still follows the hyperbolic example set by the Countach.

PARADIGM SHIFT

Its affinity to the racing car was once the source of the sports car's identity. Giannino Marzotto, who was born into a family of Italian industrialists, participated in and won the Mille Miglia in his Ferrari 195 S (1950) when he was just twenty-two – and wore a suit and tie while he did so. The Shah of Persia commissioned Carrozzeria Touring in Milan to give a Formula 1 racing car the body of a Maserati Granturismo. The result was the almighty, strange, luxurious 5000 GT (1959). Golden days! During the 1960s, motor sport underwent massive professionalisation on the one hand, while on the other hand John Cooper and Lotus-founder Colin Chapman revolutionised sports-car design with their mid-engine construction. 1960 was the last year a front-engine car won a Grand Prix. After that, Enzo Ferrari – personally the biggest fan of the front engine – found himself on the edge of bankruptcy. The era of the 'gentleman driver' was coming to a close. Tractor manufacturer and Ferrari driver Ferruccio Lamborghini, who built his first automobile in 1963, observed the emergence of a new customer base. This clientele had neither the time nor the inclination to dirty their hands with motor sport, let alone risk their lives. They preferred the playboy's life and wanted to possess the ultimate status symbol, an exotic design whose power was to be immediately visible without having to be put to the test on the racetrack. Barely drivable, barely parkable, but very striking: the Lamborghini Miura (1966) introduced the idea of the café racer. The revolution of '68, the years of terrorist threats, the oil crises, *The Limits to Growth* (1972) – a warning study on behalf of the Club of Rome that in time turned out to be completely overestimated – plunged the sports-car industry into a recession that marked the beginning of a dark decade. Between 1966 and 1970, 474 Miuras were produced; while the Countach, which came late to the market in 1974, sold just 761 in the first ten years. The political climate relaxed somewhat in the 1980s, when neo-conservative leaders – Margaret Thatcher, Ronald Reagan, Helmut Kohl – paved the way for a free-market economy. The Ferrari 288 GTO (1984) appeared just in time. Originally intended as a homologation (approval) special and easily mistaken for a tuned version of the comfortable 308 GTB, the then fastest and most powerful Ferrari every built was again given the magical acronym 'GTO', in reference to the most sought-after Ferrari 250 of all times (1962). The combination of its name and power, and the fact that it was issued as a limited edition, created a stir on the market: instead of selling 200 as planned, 272 were sold for 265,000 deutschmarks each within two years. At the same time, a grey market developed that within a year inflated the value to millions. The 288 GTO did not just found a new generation of Ferrari supercars, it also brought about a new understanding of the car as a collector's item and an object of value. As a result, 'instant classics' such as the Porsche 959 (1986), Ferrari F40 (1987), Jaguar XJ220 (1992) and their successors are hardly driven any more. Conserved in sophisticated, dust-free garages, they end up as museum objects on the one hand and as an enterprising investment on the other. Their power remains a matter of theory, for the sake of being appreciated in glossy magazines.

INTELLIGENCE

Raise the gullwing doors, step over the side panel, mind your head, tilt the steering wheel, and sit down – the Mercedes-Benz 300 SL, 1954. Turn the scissor doors, sit on the door sill, look over the roof, and park – the Lamborghini Countach, 1974. Open the butterfly doors, avoid the roof pillars, crawl into the central seat, drive off – the McLaren F1, 1993. It is incredible what drivers are forced to do in the name of ultimate design! It is possible to have stimulating arguments about the intelligence of the sports car. The correct dose of machismo, a desire for attention, and a lot of practice are still required to master even the most banal tasks on board in style. From an onlooker's perspective, all these antics are either awesome or hugely embarrassing. Even though sports cars were originally not only the fastest but also the most efficient way of getting around, off the highway, between speed bumps and toll gates, in almost every situation a Golf (post-1974) gets around more quickly. The Italian school loved to redefine the design characteristics of a certain model depending on its specific use. There were four main sports versions of the Alfa Romeo Giulietta saloon car (1955). [Fig. 6] The drop-head body by Pininfarina (1954) put everything into *bella figura*. Its line was a bonsai version of the Lancia Aurelia B24 Spider introduced by Pininfarina in the same year. The Sprint (1954), designed by Mario Felice Boano and built by Bertone, whose prototype even featured an up-swinging rear door, went for practicality: it was faster than a limousine while still family-friendly. The two-seater Sprint Speciale (1959) by Bertone, a curving, elongated design by Franco Scaglione, opted for aerodynamics and top speeds. Zagato came up with the SZ prototype in 1956, which was an extremely stripped-down version. The very compact dimensions and the light aluminium body made the exclusive production model (1960) – where no two cars were alike – unbeatable for sporting uses. Its later 'Coda Tronca' version, named after its cut-off Kammback, became a global design trendsetter. Even though they had almost identical drivetrains, each one of these Giuliettas expressed its athletic qualities in different ways: the mere concept of perfection was consistently rejected in the Italian design process. German dogma was wholly different. Since the first production automobile, the 356 (1948), the Porsche shape has been assumed correct and technically perfected with each model year. The very same shape became the basis for the design of the successor, the 901 (1963), and still lives on – though the proportions of the rear have been dramatically altered – in the 991 (2011). [Fig. 7] Doing this, Porsche allegedly announced the creation of a perfect model and the achievement of design timelessness. However, the 911 on display is not exactly the same as the 911 on the highway. The perfect shape turns out to be a mutation: a wing that automatically deploys at speeds of 80 kilometres per hour spoils the original teardrop, which is aerodynamically incapable of coping with the exaggerate power increase – V-max Type 356 = 140–170 km/h, V-max Type 991 = 283–323 km/h. It would seem the sports car of the third millennium follows the motto 'form follows myth'.

Fig. 6: Designer Elio Zagato in front of an Alfa Romeo Giulietta SZ Codatronca, 1961

PERCEPTION

A few thousand customers of exclusive sports cars and supercars on the one hand, millions of fans and billions of beholders on the other. The social history of the sports car necessarily started with its public perception in the immediate post-war period. American GIs discovered the charm of sporty cars while they were stationed in Europe and they took many back to the United States with them, generating demand there, which in turn allowed the European sports-car industry to flourish. Iconic models of the post-war era – the Alfa Romeo Giulietta Spider (1954), the Porsche 356 Speedster (1955), the BMW 507 (1956), the Mercedes 300 SL (1957) and the De Tomaso Mangusta (1967) – would not have existed in the way we know them today without the influence of people like Max Hoffman and Kjell Qvale, American car importers of Austrian and Norwegian descent respectively. The film and television industry greatly supported this development because sports cars were perfectly suited to emphasise the fame of their stars. The passenger seat was intended for their prey: be it a man as in Hitchcock's *To Catch a Thief* (1955), with Grace Kelly behind the wheel of a light blue Sunbeam Alpine Roadster (1953), or a woman as in *The Graduate* (1967), with Dustin Hoffman driving a red Alfa Romeo Spider (1966). In the TV series *The Persuaders* (1971–1972), Tony Curtis drove his Dino 246 (1969) in unceasing competition with Roger Moore's Aston Martin DBS (1967). The latter was responsible for James Bond's most famous act of infidelity in *The Spy Who Loved Me* (1977): from the British Aston Martin to the Lotus Esprit (1976), designed by Giugiaro. A later version of the Esprit brought Richard Gere and Julia Roberts together in *Pretty Woman* (1990).

Successful video games such as *The Need for Speed* (1994) and *Granturismo* (1997) subsequently brought about an epoch-making change in how sports cars are perceived. You drive alone but encounter an endless social highway via digital media. The sports car emphasises the individualism that underpins hypermodern consumerism in the third millennium. As a logical consequence, Lamborghini dared to release the Egoista single-seater (2013). In the virtual realm, every user has the ability to possess almost all models, old and new. In cyberspace, the joy of driving sports cars which are largely banned in the material world, on open roads or the best racetracks in the world, is simulated with astonishing realism for more than 200 million users. It is therefore no surprise that the most exciting sports cars are now first released in digital format to be replicated as a real vehicle later – well, perhaps. Mercedes-Benz created just a single physical replica of the AMG Vision GT (2013), the first model in the Granturismo series. Zagato celebrated the rebirth of the Italian sports-car brand IsoRivolta with a Vision GT model (2017) that had a planned 'production run' of just five vehicles. [Fig. 8] Out and about on digital roads, with a control stick instead of a steering wheel, sports cars are still what they were in Henry Ford's words right in the beginning: a toy.

1 Henry Ford, My Life and Work (1922), Gutenberg eBook edition, p. 14. http://www.gjt.bme.hu/sites/default/files/my_life_and_work_by_henry_ford_en_.pdf (accessed 26 June 2018).
2 Auto Motor und Sport, no. 19, 1984.

Fig. 7: Rear view of the Porsche 911s of 1963 and 2011
Fig. 8: Iso Rivolta Vision GT, Gran Turismo Sport, 2017

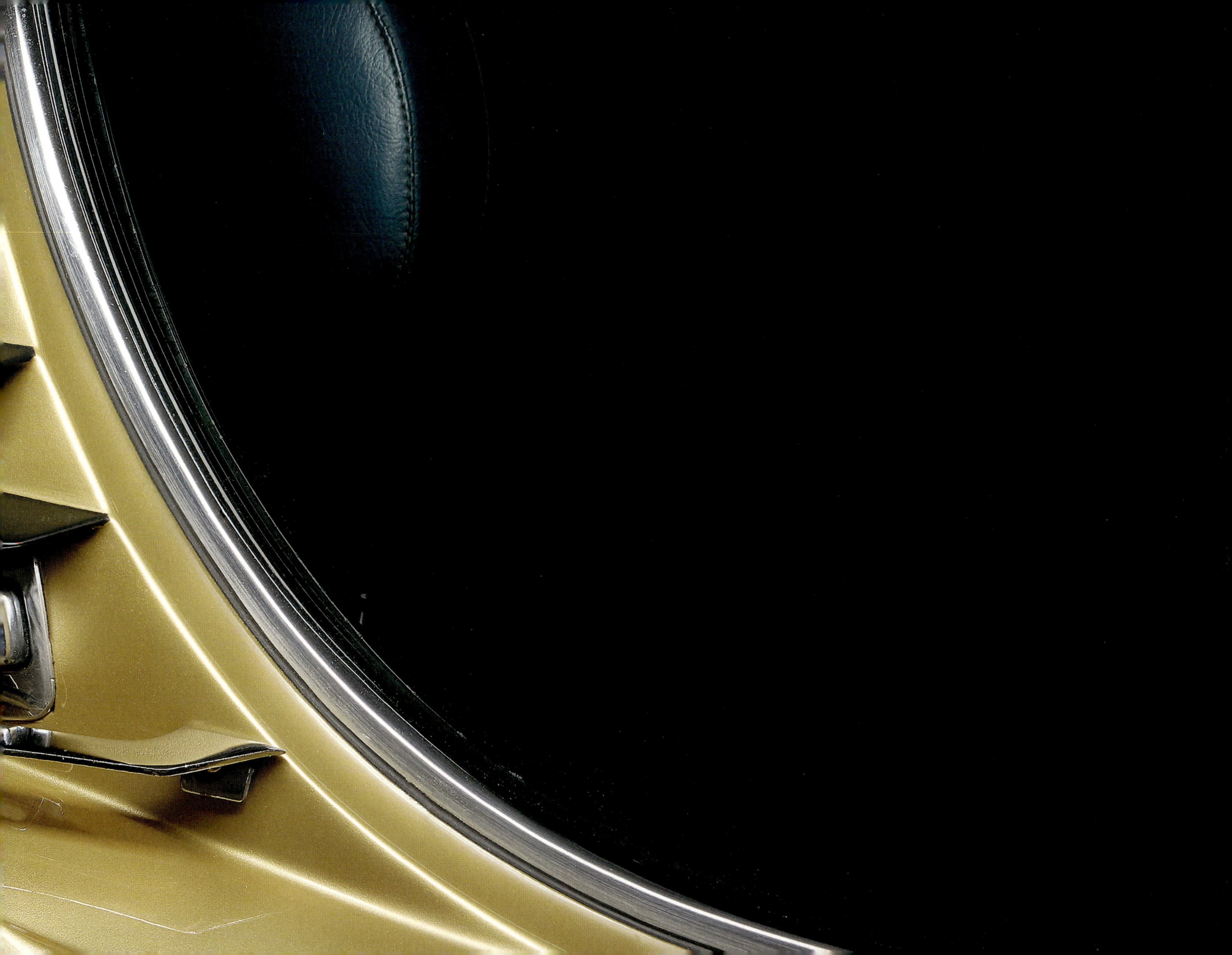

DESIGNERS AND ENGINEERS

GIOTTO BIZZARRINI (b. 1926)

After a short and varied career as lecturer and test driver, as well as a chassis and powertrain engineer, Bizzarrini, then still a young chartered engineer, left Alfa Romeo for Ferrari in 1957. In Modena, he also rose through the ranks quickly and became the lead engineer for the 250 series. Bizzarrini was involved in every aspect of the car development process: drivetrain, chassis and body engineering, as well as aerodynamics. However, regardless of his merits, Bizzarrini was ousted by Enzo Ferrari during the 'Night of the Long Knives' in 1961, whereupon he started his own business in 1962 and participated in various projects, such as the ATS 2500 sports car (designed by Franco Scaglione, built by Allemano) and the Iso models Rivolta and Grifo (both styled by Giorgetto Giugiaro). In addition, Bizzarrini designed the original Lamborghini V12 engine, known for its use in the Miura and Countach models, and produced a racing car under his own name that had initially been designed for Iso – the Bizzarrini 5300 GT Strada.

PAUL BRACQ (b. 1933)

During his tenure at the studio of designer Philippe Charbonneaux in Paris, Frenchman Bracq was conscripted and stationed in Germany. At the age of twenty-four, he embarked upon a career as designer at Mercedes-Benz, which ultimately culminated in him becoming the head of the Sindelfingen studio. Together with Mercedes chief designer, Friedrich Geiger, Bracq conceived some of the most elegant 'German' automobiles in history: the Mercedes-Benz 600, the 'Pagoda' (W113) and W111 series coupé and cabriolet. In these vehicles, Bracq combined the flair of high-quality German engineering with Mediterranean finesse, solidity with lightness – a stellar achievement, both for the Swabian make and the French designer.

His later tenures, including at BMW, where his most notable design was the BMW Turbo, and at Peugeot did not result in an oeuvre that compares favourably with that of his Stuttgart years.

ALDO BROVARONE (b. 1926)

Due to the outbreak of World War Two, Brovarone found himself unable to complete his technical and commercial studies. After the war, following a brief stint at Cisitalia, he joined Pininfarina in the mid-1950s, where he would stay until 1988. Among the many equally gifted and reticent designers of Pininfarina's second rank, Brovarone could be considered a *primus inter pares*. Whether with his own designs, such as the Dino 246, or in collaboration with his superior, Leonardo Fioravanti, Brovarone proved his sense of form to be special indeed, even among his exceptionally talented colleagues. However, Brovarone was not tied to his usual, sleek form language if circumstances demanded otherwise: hence his developing an architecturally inspired design for the Lancia Gamma Coupé in 1976. This versatility was characteristic of Brovarone, and in line with a master craftsman who never put either his own role or his style ahead of his creations or his employer.

JEAN DANINOS (1906–2001)

French-Greek Daninos was an entrepreneur, engineer and designer – all at once. It is therefore not surprising that, after having worked as an engineer on behalf of Citroën and elsewhere, Daninos ultimately founded Forges et Ateliers de Construction d'Eure et Loire – FACEL – where all his skills were needed and could be combined. Under this umbrella brand, Daninos initially manufactured aircraft components and then, after World War Two, automobile parts – at least until French automobile manufacturer Panhard withdrew its contract, which resulted in Daninos designing the first Facel Vega in 1954.

This and all subsequent models were created by Daninos in order to precisely suit his personal preferences. Which was not surprising, as he himself was an extravagant, style-conscious, affluent entrepreneur and therefore perfectly in tune with the target group for his grande *routière*. However, Daninos did not know much about the mass market, which is why failure of the cheaper Facellia model ultimately brought about the end of the company in 1964.

LEONARDO FIORAVANTI (b. 1938)

Ferraris were Fioravanti's speciality. An engineer as well as an equally talented and passionate amateur racing driver, he oversaw the design of a wide range of vehicles during his long and successful career at Pininfarina, where he rose through the ranks, all the way to that of chief designer. However, the icons from Maranello – especially the 365 GTB/4 Daytona and the 365 GT4 2+2, which Fioravanti personally designed – remain most closely associated with his name. At the same time, there are many classics among the Ferrari models he oversaw, but which were created by other designers. Bearing this in mind, Fioravanti's move to Ferrari for a brief period after he had left Pininfarina in 1988 made perfect sense. As a good designer, but first and foremost as the manager of a team of outstanding stylists, Fioravanti therefore earned himself a special place in the annals of Pininfarina and Ferrari.

MARCELLO GANDINI (b. 1938)

Being a taciturn misfit, as well as scion of a well-off family, gave Gandini enough self-confidence and stubbornness, even at a young age, to become one of the driving forces behind a revolution in automotive design. As successor to his equally brilliant predecessor Giorgetto Giugiaro in the role of chief designer at Bertone, Gandini, who was not even thirty at that time, only briefly seized on Giugiaro's achievements (Lamborghini Miura). Then he quickly developed a completely unique, groundbreaking and wildly avant-garde style that he then refined over the course of a ludicrously creative decade of celestial designs (Bertone's Carabo, Stratos Zero, Marzal and many more), whose significance for automotive design in general cannot be overstated.

However, as with every success story, Gandini's period of boundless creativity proved to be finite, which is why he failed to reach his previous creative heights – which had been truly dizzying indeed – again, from the late-1970s onwards.

FRIEDRICH GEIGER (1907–1996)

This long-serving and significant Mercedes designer was actually a native of Swabia. First as an employee, then as head of the department still known as *Stilistik* at the time, Geiger shaped the forms of cars produced under the three-pointed star between 1933 and 1973. He was involved in the design of the famous 540K and the legendary 300 SL, for which he developed a number of elements that were seminal and helped to define the brand. Such as the 300 SL's gullwing doors and the *Sport* grille, which were both conceived under Geiger. In his role as chief designer, Geiger also oversaw and supervised the work of Paul Bracq and his own future successor, Bruno Sacco.

Until the late 1970s, all Mercedes models hence bore Geiger's handwriting – sometimes with an elegant French twist (as with Bracq's creations), sometimes featuring avant-garde references (like the C111), and sometimes in lavishly baroque fashion (in the case of the 1970s' production models) – the constant being an unerring flair of Swabian virtuousness.

GIORGETTO GIUGIARO (b. 1938)

Beginning his career as a draftsman when he was an adolescent, Giugiaro, the son of a fresco painter, soon rapidly rose through the ranks to become a designer. Thanks to the patronage of 'Nuccio' Bertone, Giugiaro was appointed Bertone's chief designer in his early twenties, succeeding Franco Scaglione, whereupon he immediately created a concept car – the Testudo – that was to remain influential for more than two decades. He then worked at Ghia, before finally setting up his own design studio, Italdesign.

At his company he then developed the wedge shape – in parallel with Marcello Gandini – as well as the 'folded paper' aesthetic, which he bestowed upon creations such as the Lotus Esprit and the Golf Mk1 during the 1970s. Once automotive shapes became softer again, Giugiaro was once more at the forefront of this movement. Furthermore, he was fascinated with the functional use of space, an interest most keenly demonstrated with his Fiat Panda from 1980, the ultimate utilitarian, rational automobile – and Giugiaro's own favourite design.

ALBRECHT GRAF VON GOERTZ (1914–2006)

The German aristocrat Count Albrecht von Goertz emigrated to the United States in 1936, where he made his way into automotive design through his hobby – tinkering with Hot Rods. Having joined exceptionally successful designer Raymond Loewy, von Goertz was commissioned to work on behalf of Studebaker, before he became a freelancer and met North American BMW importer Max Hoffman. After Hoffman had paved the way for von Goertz, the Count was assigned to design the BMW 507 and 503 models, which came to the market in 1955. The German-American subsequently worked sporadically as a consultant for Japanese car manufacturers. However, only in the case of the gorgeous Nissan Silvia CSP311 Coupé has von Goertz's involvement remained uncontested. In many other instances, such as those of the smash hit Datsun 240 Z and the Toyota 2000 GT, von Goertz was falsely credited with their respective designs, sometimes for years.

WILLIAM HEYNES (1904–1989)

When William 'Bill' Munger Heynes was hired by William Lyons in 1935 to become chief engineer for SS Cars, nobody could have foreseen the kind of career he would look back upon in 1969, when Heynes retired as chief engineer of Jaguar (as SS Cars called itself after the end of the World War Two). The motor cars developed under Heynes, and in collaboration with significant engineers such as Bob Knight, Walter Hassan, Harry Mundy and Malcolm Sayer, were the vehicles that turned SS Cars into Jaguar, and therefore transformed a British niche business into a marque of global repute. The XK six-cylinder engine in particular, which was designed during wartime, when the engineers were on fire-watch duty during the Blitz, proved crucial, as it powered sports cars (XK120, E-type), saloons (Mark VII, Mk2, XJ6) and race cars (C-type, D-type). The latter two vehicles, which turned out to be victorious at Le Mans, were most strongly influenced by racing enthusiast Heynes.

ERWIN KOMENDA (1904–1966)

The Beetle-like *Ur*-aesthetic of the German automobile, as expressed, at varying heights, through vehicles like the Volkswagen Type 1, as well as the Porsche 356 and 911 models, was conceived by the Austrian body engineer and designer Erwin Komenda. Between 1931 and 1966, first under Ferdinand Porsche and then his son, 'Ferry' Porsche, Komenda ran the body engineering department. There, he went about constantly optimising the ideal shape of the rear-wheel-driven two-door car. To this end, he would sometimes integrate the wings, or lend the body a smoother appearance, in order to improve upon the vehicle's motor sports performance. However, he always remained loyal to the fundamental shape of the round rear. Whether Komenda was inspired to create this basic design by drawing on the groundbreaking streamline cars devised by the Czech company Tatra is a question that still fuels speculation today.

WILLIAM LYONS (1901–1985)

The significance of design to the Jaguar brand is demonstrated by the fact that this is the only production-car manufacturer whose founder also acted as its chief designer. An autodidact in that regard, Sir William allowed himself to be inspired by the competition (particularly from Italy), yet at the same time he would always trust his own, unerring taste. The low, elegant, striking, but never vulgar lines that turned a Jaguar into a cat among automobiles could always be traced back to the boss himself, even though he was barely capable of drawing a straight line. Thanks to the outstanding tinsmiths who translated his ideas into metal shapes and the brilliant engineers at his side, Coventry thus became the hometown of enormously graceful sports cars and saloons – and it was the latter that were the true passion of Sir William, who considered his final design for the XJ saloon his best effort.

GIOVANNI MICHELOTTI (1921–1980)

Being a particularly enterprising freelance automotive designer, Michelotti ended up shaping car design of the 1950s to the 1970s like few others. After an apprenticeship at Farina, he worked mainly on behalf of Carrozzeria Alfredo Vignale, where he created a number of Maserati and Ferrari designs. However, Michelotti was also responsible for numerous models produced by a range of mass manufacturers. In that context, his impact was most obvious on the British Standard Triumph brand, as Michelotti acted as that company's (freelance) chief designer. In addition, he also worked for the Japanese make Hino, advised BMW during its reorientation after the Bavarian company's near-bankruptcy, and designed various models (including lorries) on behalf of DAF.

FERDINAND ALEXANDER PORSCHE (1935–2012)

Rather than following in the footsteps of his father and grandfather, who were both engineers, F. A., known as 'Butzi' Porsche, 'Ferry' Porsche's son, opted for a career as a designer. He attended (albeit briefly) the Hochschule für Gestaltung in Ulm, an incredibly influential academic establishment at the time, which was headed by Otl Aicher, among others. Then, in 1957, 'Butzi' started work at Porsche's design department under Erwin Komenda. It was there that 'Butzi' created his most famous work, the Porsche 911, which clearly betrays Ulmer Schule influences, such as the renunciation of what was deemed unnecessary and faddish. The *Elfer* ultimately remained F. A. Porsche's only road vehicle design, as he, like all family members, had to resign from his active post at the company in 1972. 'Butzi' subsequently founded his own studio – Porsche Design – in Austria, which focused on product design.

BRUNO SACCO (b. 1933)

In the case of Italian-born Bruno Sacco, it would be foolish to try and sum up his achievements through any single car design. For the long-standing Mercedes chief designer's talents did not so much lie in the styling side of the craft, but in conceptual work and team leadership. Thanks to decades of work (including as the project manager for the Mercedes C111), Sacco had commended himself to such an extent that he was considered a worthy successor to long-time chief designer, Friedrich Geiger. Having attained the top post, Sacco invested many years of research and thought into a concept known as Vertical Affinity/Horizontal Homogeneity, a kind of institutionalised timelessness in design and function. And indeed, the Mercedes models designed in accordance with these parameters and unveiled between 1979 and 1989 can truly be considered the pinnacle of – in the best sense – 'German' automotive design. For in these cars, Sacco combined principles of the Ulmer Schule with the ideals embodied by Mercedes, which resulted in a generation of vehicles of immense design quality that remains relevant today.

MALCOLM SAYER (1916–1970)

No other automotive designer used quite the same *modus operandi* as trained aerodynamicist Malcolm Sayer did at Jaguar. Using mathematical formulae that were completely incomprehensible to everyone else, he calculated the aerodynamic efficiency of his designs, before testing them by taping pieces of cotton wool attached to strings to the various prototypes. Sayer would then observe their 'flight characteristics' while driving alongside in another vehicle. Legendary race cars, such as the C-type and D-type models, were created this way, as well as the iconic Jaguar E-type. Sayer, having been earmarked as the successor to Sir William Lyons as Jaguar's chief designer, was working on the design of the Jaguar XJ-S when he unexpectedly died – a car that barely resembles the E-type, but whose controversial rear sail panels are as aerodynamically justified as the curvaceous hips of Sayer's undisputed masterpiece.

FRANCO SCAGLIONE (1916–1993)

'Nuccio' Bertone's unparalleled instinct for finding creative talent was proven for the first time in 1951, when he hired illustrator and war veteran Franco Scaglione to work as a designer for his company. At Bertone, Scaglione rapidly developed a style of his own: aerodynamics-focused, yet also fearless when it came to combining decorative opulence with streamlined elegance. The pinnacle of this creative period were the prototypes of the Berlinetta Aerodinamica Tecnica (B.A.T. for short) series, which were jointly developed by Alfa Romeo and Bertone. With these three B.A.T. designs, Scaglione instantly established Bertone as a stylistic pioneer. These cars, which constituted an amalgamation of a Le Mans race car, an American rocket concept vehicle and a Jules Verne fantasy, were to remain Scaglione's calling card when he set up his own company in 1959. At least until he thrilled the design world one last time with the equally spectacular, but more purist Alfa Romeo 33 Stradale in 1967.

ERCOLE SPADA (b. 1938)

Like that of many of his peers, Spada's career as an automotive designer began when he was an adolescent, without any professional training, in 1960. And yet he instantly went about creating classics, such as the Aston Martin DB4 GT Zagato and the Lancia Flamina Super Sport Zagato, in his role as Zagato's chief designer, which he held until 1969. Later on, Spada would work on behalf of very different companies, such as Ghia, Audi and BMW (where he was involved in designing the highly influential 1986 7 Series saloon), before he was hired by the I.DE.A design institute in 1983, which was followed by another brief stint at Zagato. It was not just his career path that was rather curious, though, but also the fact that he dismissed his most famous, most successful creations as too conventional, much preferring idiosyncratic designs such as the Lancia Fulvia Sport's himself.

RUDOLF UHLENHAUT (1906–1989)

The role of Anglo-German Uhlenhaut amidst the fierce competition between Auto Union and Mercedes-Benz for dominance in European pre-war racing was special indeed. Not just due to his ancestry, Uhlenhaut must be considered an exceptional player within that Fascism-tinged world of motor sports. In addition, his talents as a driver eclipsed many a Silver Arrow race driver's. However, since Uhlenhaut's skills as an engineer were even more pronounced, his focus remained on the technical side, where he achieved major successes. After the war, Uhlenhaut continued on this path and later designed the Mercedes 300 SL race car. Which not only won at Le Mans, but was also used as the basis for the 300 SL 'gullwing' production car. The Mercedes 300 SLR on the other hand was a road-legal race car built just twice, for Uhlenhaut personally, which the engineer would use as a racy everyday car throughout his life.

KARL WILFERT (1907–1976)

As chief engineer at Mercedes-Benz, Austrian Karl Wilfert's influence on the company proved formative for more than five decades, starting in 1936. Alongside the legendary Béla Barényi, he revolutionised vehicle safety, way beyond the Stuttgart-based company itself. For Mercedes-Benz' research in this field at the time was of truly fundamental nature. Wilfert also worked closely with the chief development engineer Rudolf Uhlenhaut. In addition, he was responsible for the styling department, where his counterparts were Friedrich Geiger, Paul Bracq and Bruno Sacco. Since engineering and safety-related aspects were given particular attention in Mercedes-Benz's automotive designs at the time, the work done by Wilfert and his engineering staff left a clear mark on the aesthetics of the company and its products. Even after Wilfert's retirement, this formative legacy was still maintained by his successor, Werner Breidtschwert.

COACHBUILDERS AND DESIGN STUDIOS

ALLEMANO

Founded in Turin as a car repair shop by Serafino Allemano in 1928, Carrozzeria Allemano started manufacturing complete car bodies, mostly for Fiat and Lancia, in 1935. After the end of the war, the company also began to build bodies for foreign manufacturers; however, the majority of Allemano's creations continued to be based on Italian chassis. Some of these designs were created in collaboration with Giovanni Michelotti, including that for the Maserati 5000 GT, which still remains the best-known Allemano work. However, not even this moderate financial success was enough to prevent Allemano, like many other *carrozzieri*, from losing its business model as a result of the transition from body-on-frame to monocoque car-body construction. Eventually, Allemano closed down in 1965.

BERTONE

Founded by Giovanni Bertone in Turin in 1912 as a business for manufacturing carriages, the company rapidly switched to building car bodies. Thanks to a good rapport with, among others, Vincenzo Lancia, Bertone was able to expand until the outbreak of the First World War. Even during the war, production was maintained, albeit on a small scale.

The most significant chapter in Bertone's history started in 1950, though, when Giovanni's son, Giuseppe, known as 'Nuccio', took over the business, and series production of the Alfa Romeo Giulietta and Sprint Coupés started. This step established Bertone as a contract manufacturer of complete vehicles on the one hand; on the other, the Franco Scaglione-designed Giulietta Sprint also demonstrated the company's styling competence. These two departments – manufacturing and styling – remained Bertone's pillars of success for decades, and were only surpassed by Nuccio Bertone's ability to nurture exceptionally gifted designers, such as the aforementioned Franco Scaglione, not to mention Giorgetto Giugiaro and Marcello Gandini later on. However, after having parted ways with the latter, Bertone was unable to recruit similarly exceptional talent as a replacement. And once contract production became less attractive for automobile manufacturers around the new millennium, Bertone's ultimate decline set in, eventually ending in bankruptcy in 2014.

GHIA

Under founder Giacinto Ghia, the *carrozzeria* mostly designed and built race cars based on Italian chassis between 1916 and the start of the Second World War. From 1944 onwards, Ghia's business model and style changed substantially, however. Especially under the leadership of Luigi Segre and chief designer Pietro Frua, Ghia drew inspiration from the then leading American designers, which did not just attract US makes such as Lincoln and Chrysler, but also led to commissions from companies such as VW (Karmann Ghia) and Volvo. Despite the hiring of industry greats like Giorgetto Giugiaro and Tom Tjaarda as chief designers later on, Ghia's repeated changes of ownership ultimately led to its takeover by Ford, which heralded the slow decline and eventual end of this Turinese design studio.

PININFARINA

Pininfarina is greater than any one designer. This is the motto of the *carrozzeria* that produced such illustrious names as Franco Martinengo, Aldo Brovarone, Tom Tjaarda, Paolo Martin, Enrico Fumia, Leonardo Fioravanti and Ken Okuyama, but did not single out any of them for a long period of time. For Pininfarina was never shaped by the genius of an individual, as was true for Bertone or Giugiaro's Italdesign; instead, this *carrozzeria* embodied the stylistic legacy of Battista 'Pinin' Farina.

Having learned the coachbuilding trade from his older brother, Giovanni Farina, at his company, Stabilimenti Farina, Battista set up shop on his own under his nickname 'Pinin' ('the youngest') in 1930 and became the first coachbuilder to adapt the construction of monocoque bodies. Later on, 'Pinin' established a fertile partnership with Ferrari that was to last for more than sixty years. Thanks to 'Pinin's' unerring eye, flawless elegance eventually became the heart and soul of Carrozzeria Pininfarina.

When 'Pinin's' son, Sergio Pininfarina, took over reigns in 1961 (the same year both family and company changed their name), this core aspect remained intact, even though the young Pininfarina was not a designer himself. Instead, he proved to be an incredibly prudent helmsman of the company, whose influence contributed to all those brilliant designers delivering their best work while at Pininfarina.

With Sergio Pininfarina's departure, the company lost exactly this kind of leadership, but was ultimately able to avoid bankruptcy, not least thanks to its still excellent reputation.

SCAGLIETTI

Craftsmanship and an instinctive sense for aesthetics ensured that, from the 1950s onwards, Sergio Scaglietti's automobile repair shop moved away from merely repairing to an excellent standard, the Ferraris that had been damaged on the racetrack. Instead, Scaglietti began designing and building new models for its neighbour in Modena. These vehicles were largely race cars, but sometimes also road cars, in some cases designed by Pininfarina, in others conceived of by Scaglietti himself. His *modus operandi* resembled that of many a design autodidact: he built what he considered beautiful, without drawings or blueprints. For this, he received personal approval from Enzo Ferrari, who also ensured that Carrozzeria Scaglietti did not get left by the wayside when Ferrari was taken over by Fiat, but was also incorporated.

TOURING

Few *carrozzieri* have changed as much over time as Touring, which was established in Milan in 1926. Under the leadership of its founder, Felice Bianchi Anderloni, the focus of this company during the pre- and early post-war period was on race vehicles, for which the delicate and light '*superleggera*' construction method was invented; it combined the stability of a tubular frame with the light weight of an aluminium skin. Carlo Felice Bianchi Anderloni, the founder's son and his successor from 1948 onwards, initially maintained this business model, but increasingly repositioned Touring in the sector of glamorous designs for *gran turismo coupés* during the mid-1950s. Touring's design for the Aston Martin DB4, 5 and 6 became particularly well known. However, by the early 1960s, the company started to lose its touch with the stylistic *zeitgeist*. And since the body-on-frame construction method became obsolete at the same time, Touring had to cease production in 1966.

ZAGATO

Zagato holds a special place among the *carrozzieri*, and not just because the company has been owned by the same family for almost a century. It is also due to a unique, unmistakable style, whose origins lie in pre-war racing and company founder Ugo Zagato's early interest in aerodynamics. This approach was further developed under Ugo's son Elio during the 1950s, insofar as Zagato produced lighter and, more importantly, faster versions of a number of different sports cars (by Aston Martin, Osca, Maserati and others). This resulted in an unmistakable aesthetic, which, in its most extreme permutation, led to the Fiat-Abarth 750 Zagato with its double bubble roof and brash wings. Under chief designer Ercole Spada, the style of Zagato's output became more professional from 1950 onwards, yet hardly less eccentric. It is not least because the family-run company has stayed true to this headstrong approach that Zagato still exists today.

This publication accompanies the exhibition

CARS – DRIVEN BY DESIGN SPORTS CARS FROM THE 1950S TO THE 1970S

Kunstpalast
27 September 2018 to 10 February 2019

KUNST PALAST

EXHIBITION KUNSTPALAST

Curators: Barbara Til and Dieter Castenow
Project head: Bianca Raitz-Tinzmann
Project assistant: Yasmin Limbach
Registrar: Dorothea Nutt
Intern: Nina Geisen

Conservation and restoration consultants: Die Schmiede

CATALOGUE

Editors: Barbara Til and Dieter Castenow
Project assistants: Elke Dichter, Christiane Jungklaus, Yasmin Limbach, Maria Zinser
Catalogue management: Bianca Raitz-Tinzmann

Project head Hirmer: Kerstin Ludolph
Project management Hirmer: Jutta Allekotte
Copy-editor (German): Katrin Boskamp-Priever, Bremen
English translation: Christopher Butt, Hamburg (catalogue entries and biographies); Josephine Cordero-Sapien, Exeter; Michael Scuffil, Leverkusen
English copy-editor: Chris Murray, Nantwich
Design: Sophie Friederich
Typesetting: Gunnar Musan

Printed in Germany

The Deutsche Nationalbibliothek lists this publication in the Deutschen Nationalbibliografie; detailed bibliographic information is available on the Internet at http://www.dnb.de

German museum edition:
ISBN 978-3-86832-447-1

German trade edition:
ISBN 978-3-7774-3123-9

English trade edition:
ISBN 978-3-7774-3122-2

www.hirmerpublishers.com

Front cover: Lamborghini Miura S Serie II, 1970 (p. 106), photo: Oliver Sold

Back cover: Lamborghini Miura P400, 1968 (p. 106, side view with open boot and bonnet), photo: Oliver Sold

Frontispiece, p. 2: Ferrari 250 GT SWB (p. 74, rear), photo: Oliver Sold; p. 3: BMW Turbo, 1972, (p. 134, back part of roof), photo: Oliver Sold; p. 4: BMW 507 Factory Prototype, 1955 (p. 58, rear), photo: Oliver Sold; p. 5: Aston Martin DB4 GT Zagato, 1962 (p. 78, petrol cap)

Display pages: De Tomaso Mangusta, 1967 (p. 114, rear), photo: Oliver Sold; pp. 10/11: Cisitalia 202 SC Berlinetta, 1948 (p. 34, right side, rear fender), photo: Oliver Sold; p. 12: Alfa Romeo Giulietta Sprint Speciale (SS) Prototipo Bertone, 1957 (p. 62, front fender), photo: © Carrstudio / Collezione Lopresto; p. 20: Ferrari 250 GT SWB Berlinetta Competizione, 1961 (p. 74, rear), photo: Oliver Sold; pp. 32/33: Porsche 911, 1966 (p. 94, rear), photo: Oliver Sold; pp. 146/147: Cisitalia 202 SC Berlinetta, 1948 (p. 34, left front fender), photo: Oliver Sold; p. 148: Lamborghini Miura P400, 1968 (p. 106, headlamp), photo: Oliver Sold; p. 156: BMW Turbo, 1972, radiator grille (p. 134, 'BMW kidney'), photo: Oliver Sold; pp. 166/167: Lamborghini Miura P400, 1968 (p. 106, air inlet over door handle), photo: Oliver Sold; p. 178: Mercedes-Benz C111 Typ II, 1970 (p. 130, interior), photo: © Mercedes-Benz Classic

PHOTO CREDITS

p. 14 © Official SpaceX Photos | p. 15 © Fonds de Dotation Peugeot pour la Mémoire de l'Histoire industrielle | pp. 16, 63–65 © Carrstudio / Collezione Lopresto | pp. 16, 44, 96, 165 © Porsche Werkfoto | pp. 17, 131–133, 158 © Mercedes-Benz Classic | p. 18 © Les Films 13 – Claude Lelouch | p. 22 Hampel Fine Art Auctions GmbH & Co KG | p. 22 Universitäts-bibliothek Heidelberg, Iconologia di Cesare Ripa, p. 645 – CC-BY-SA 3.0 | p. 23 Photo by Philippe Le Tellier/Jack Garofalo/Paris Match via Getty Images | p. 24 Studiocanal | pp. 25, 35–37, 39–41, 47–49, 51–53, 55–57, 59–61, 67–69, 71–73, 75–77, 87–89, 91–93, 95–97, 99–101, 103–105, 107–113, 115, 117, 123–125, 127–129, 135–137, 139–141, 143–145, photo: Oliver Sold | pp. 26, 144 © Automobili Lamborghini | p. 27 photo: Dirk de Jager © 2016, p. 152 photo: Eric Fuller © 2017 Courtesy of RM Sotheby's | p. 28 photostudio Bartsch, Karen Bartsch, Berlin / Grisebach GmbH | p. 29 Kunstbibliothek, Staatliche Museen zu Berlin © bpk / Kunstbibliothek, SMB / Dietmar Katz | p. 30 © imago/Granata Images | p. 36 Copyright unknown. Photographic Archive. The Museum of Modern Art Archives, New York. Cat. no.: IN488.1 DIGITAL IMAGE © 2018, The Museum of Modern Art, New York/ Scala, Florence | p. 36 © Pininfarina | pp. 44, 48, 132 © Automuseum PROTOTYP, Hamburg | pp. 43–45 Autostadt GmbH | pp. 56, 68 photo: Edward Quinn, © edwardquinn.com | p. 60 photo: Jean-Marie Bottequin, p. 136 © BMW Group Archiv | pp. 72, 116, 159, 162 © Quattroruote Archives, Courtesy Goodbrands Institute for Automotive Culture | pp. 80, 164, 165 © Archive A. Zagato | pp. 83–85 photo: Michel Zumbrunn | p. 84 © JDHT | p. 100 Centro Documentazione Alfa Romeo – Arese | pp. 116, 153, 154 © Quattroruote Archives | pp. 119–121 Toyota Deutschland GmbH | p. 120 Film still from the James Bond film *You Only Live Twice*, 1967 | p. 124 http://www.hdbilder.eu/p/189123/2048/1152 | p. 150 Centro Storico Fiat | p. 150 photo: © Michael Furman | p. 151 General Motors | p. 160 © Archivio Prospero Gian-ferrari, Public Domain | p. 161 © Pininfarina; Courtesy Goodbrands Institute for Automotive Culture

It was not always possible to identify the owners of the rights to the illustrations. Justified claims will of course be recognised in the framework of the usual agreements.

KUNSTPALAST

Board
Felix Krämer, Harry Schmitz
Cornelia Brüggemann, Dorothee von Deutsch, Felicity Korn

Deputy Heads, Collections, Sculpture and Applied Art
Barbara Til
Elke Dichter, Christiane Jungklaus, Inge Maruyama, Maria Zinser

Paintings
Bettina Baumgärtel
Hanna Bahr

Modern Art
Kay Heymer
Anne Rodler

Glass Museum Hentrich
Dedo von Kerssenbrock-Krosigk
Caroline Blume

Prints and Drawings
Gunda Luyken
Sonja Brink, Melanie Grimm, Claudia Petersen, Bertram Rutz

Library
Sabine Schroyen

Exhibition management
Sandra Badelt
Corinna Gramatke, Yasmin Limbach, Theresa Nink, Dorothea Nutt, Bianca Raitz-Tinzmann, Svenja Schütte, Sophie-Marie Sümmermann

Infrastructure and exhibition technology
Andreas Nabrotzky
Meik Andrysiak, Georg Buddrus, Bastian Erhard, Sven Hager, Jan Knobloch, Lothar Milatz, Roland Mönninghoff, Fred Schlegel, Eberhard Schollmeyer

Education
Birgit van de Water
Alina Fuchte, Birgit Huebner, Miriam von Gehren, Steffen Krautzig, Sabine Parsow, Dagmar Vennhaus

Marketing and Digital
Christian Hupertz
Christine Böhm, Verena Crolla, Claudia Gutberlet-Zieburg

Press
Marina Schuster
Christina Bolius

Controlling
Susanne Schambach

Bookkeeping
Peter Maas
Petra Hecht, Isabelle Ruthe

Human Resources
Karin Eichberg
Marion Kallen, Esther Webers

Museum shop
Marcella von Uthmann-Gillessen
Karina Kullmann

Robert-Schumann-Saal
Eckart Schulze-Neuhoff
Ulla Baumeister

Freunde des Kunstpalastes
Jantien Bierich

Conservation
Restaurierungszentrum der Landeshauptstadt Düsseldorf / Schenkung Henkel

Stiftung Museum Kunstpalast
Ehrenhof 4–5
40479 Düsseldorf
www.kunstpalast.de

The exhibition is sponsored by

GRAND BASEL

BENTLEY
BENTLEY DÜSSELDORF

CHRISTIE'S

DENEKE GMBH
Versicherungsmakler

Gothaer

TÜVRheinland®
Genau. Richtig.

Süddeutsche Zeitung

WDR 3

Düsseldorf
Nähe trifft Freiheit